Sexual Shame
An Urgent Call to Healing

Karen A. McClintock

Fortress Press

Minneapolis

SEXUAL SHAME
An Urgent Call to Healing

Cover art: "Autumn Nostalgia (Orange Lady)" by Alexander Semyonov (1997). Copyright © Krasnaya/SuperStock. Used by permission.
Cover design: Marti Naughton
Interior design: Beth Wright

Scripture quotations are from the New Revised Standard Version Bible, copyright © 1989 by the Division of Christian Education of the National Council of the Churches of Christ in the USA, and are used by permission.

Library of Congress Cataloging-in-Publication Data

McClintock, Karen A., date—
    Sexual shame : an urgent call to healing / Karen A. McClintock.
        p.   cm.
    Includes bibliographical references.
    ISBN 0-8006-3238-9 (alk. paper)
    1. Sex—Religious aspects—Christianity. 2. Shame—Religious aspects—
Christianity. I. Title
    BT708 .M42 2001
    241'.66—dc21

                                                        00-065410

The paper used in this publication meets the minimum requirements of American National Standard for Information Sciences — Permanence of Paper for Printed Library Materials, ANSI Z329.48-1984.

Manufactured in the U.S.A.   AF 1-3238
05   04   03   02   01   1   2   3   4   5   6   7   8   9   10

Contents

Preface

The Many Faces of Sexual Shame

Perhaps you have picked up this book because you have experienced sexual shame. The feeling of shame underlies sexual dysfunction: impotence, lack of sexual drive, sexual compulsion, and incest. The experience of sexual shame underlies obesity in women and contributes to anorexia and bulimia. Sexual shame in men may be experienced as impotence, depression, and addiction. Sexual identity shame is at the core of the hiding or "closets" that gay people and their families often live in. Sexual shame affects individuals, families, congregations, and communities.

Sexual shame erodes individual self-esteem, relational health, and congregational life. The parents of gay sons feel shame. People who don't live up to their own ideals as perfect lovers feel shame. Christians who live in committed partnerships without the contract of marriage feel shame about "living in sin" in the eyes of the church. Congregations that restrict conversation about sexuality or repress it with taboos and stigmatization remain shame-bound.

Within each community and congregation there are members who have been living in deep shame. Shame may be reinforced through preaching and teaching about immorality and sin. Shame may be underneath an individual's hesitance to become active in a congregation. Shame may be the reason someone sneaks into the back row and sneaks out to the parking lot hoping not to be noticed.

This book is offered as a resource for congregational discussion and for the personal liberation of those who have experienced shame in their families or in the church. I write it believing that we are all created in God's image, male and female, and that we were intended from the time of creation to live without shame. When God created the first man and the first woman, they were created in God's perfect image. They were also "both naked, and [they] were not ashamed" (Gen. 2:25).

Some of the stories you will find in this text may produce discomfort. The experience of shame is deep and can become overwhelming.

I encourage you to talk with someone about reading this book and to invite dialogue with others in a church study or meeting. If you experience repressed memories or painful feelings as you read these stories, you are encouraged to call your local church or mental health help-line and seek support.

Stories of Personal Shame

A woman told me that her grandmother tried to drown her in the bathtub when she was three.

"Why?" I asked.

"Because I was the bastard child. My mother wasn't married to my father. She was married to someone else. It shamed the whole family. My grandmother wanted it all to go away. She wanted me dead, and then they could go on as if it never happened."

The mother's sexual shame was borne out upon the child. All of her life the grandmother tortured her, forced her to eat too much, and then called her a "fat, ugly slob"—forcing her to live in shame.

Jenny started running away from her family home when she was eight. Her stepfather often beat her. He wore big steel-toed work boots and kicked her with them—on the legs, in the groin, in the face after she had fallen down. To get away she fled to her older cousin's house, where she was able to live a quieter life. The cousin would play games with her and wrestle with her. When they wrestled, he'd start touching her. He'd ask her to sit on his lap when he had erections. That's how it started. And it got worse.

Jenny coped with it all by imagining herself to be a princess and him the prince. She imagined that someday he'd marry her. When she grew up, he told her, she would be his forever. He wouldn't beat her or hurt her like her stepfather had. They would live happily ever after.

Jenny goes to church on Sunday and sings in the choir. Then she goes home and struggles with depression and physical pain. No one knows this about her. There is nowhere in the church for her to begin her healing. She is ashamed of her past. She is ashamed that she doesn't even have any sexual impulses as an adult. Yet somehow she experiences in church a little bit of God's grace, a little bit of love. The congregation members look at her and just think to themselves, "She's rather strange." She doesn't get invited to potlucks in people's homes. She imagines that none of the others who go to church could be as "bad" as she is.

Bill wants to be a better father and husband, and he asks for a Christian therapist. He wants to know how to improve his relationship with his wife. He talks about his marriage, his work, and his low-level depression. With a sadness I haven't seen in our first few sessions, he nervously says to me, "I think we need to have a little more romance." "Okay," I ask, "what are some romantic things you'd like to do?" We make a list, but he is still restless. My intuition tells me that he can go deeper. "Would you feel comfortable telling me what your sex life is like?" He shifts a bit in the chair. "Well, it's . . . you know, umm . . . we don't do it very often. Sometimes it's just fast and, like, we just do because, well, you know, I need to." He's shaking his head side to side. "Not very satisfying?" I asked. He has cast his eyes downward. They are glued to the floor. He quietly says, "No." As we explore this further, I realize that he is ashamed of his own needs, ashamed of the way he uses his wife to release the tension but doesn't really exchange pleasure with her. He so obviously values sexual intimacy, but he hasn't learned how to achieve it. His shame falls into the gap between the pleasurable mutual sexuality that he longs for and the fast release of physical tension that he engages in.

Jackie confesses her sins to her priest every two weeks, those she has committed and those she is thinking about committing. She finds the ritual healing. She also finds the purity and chastity of the orders of priests and nuns comforting. In fact, she has thought once or twice about becoming a nun. After all, she has spent her life giving her body to men who abuse her. It isn't what she wanted, but it is what she was taught. When Jackie was five, her father left the family. Her mother had no work skills and three young children to raise. Every man who came along was suitable. She didn't have the resources to be picky, and she had little discretion in her pursuit to get a man to stay with her. Sometimes Jackie stood in the doorway of her mother's room and watched her have sex with a new man in the hope that, this time, the man would pay their rent. What Jackie saw wasn't full of tender exchange, and she was frightened that her mother would be hurt or would die. She was frozen in observation of a scene unlike anything else she knew. She tried to forget it during the week, wearing her blue pleated skirt and white blouse at school. At church everyone was pure, and no one had sex or talked about sex. It was safe for her there. Jackie's mother never taught her the difference between mature, loving sexuality and lying on your back so that a man might pay the bills. The power of the family overwhelmed the silence of the church, and the tension remained. Jackie's shame falls between the fantasy of celibate devotion and the reality of prostituted security.

These are not extreme situations or fabricated life stories (though the names and details have been changed to protect their anonymity). If you haven't heard anyone tell stories like these, it is because of the strong taboos about speaking these truths to anyone. Families have silenced these stories for the preservation of their esteem. Their silence protects them from change and, in some cases, arrest and conviction. These are a few of the stories of persons who worship with you on any Sunday. These persons need words of healing and hope. They need to know of Christ's love and grace; they need to be reminded that they are no more stuck in their abusive past than Moses and his people were stuck in Egypt when they gave their lives over to God and asked to be led to the promised land.

When the topic of sexual shame is opened up, lots of conversation can begin. Colleagues who are aware that I am writing on this subject have sought me out to tell the stories of their own shame and shaming experiences. They tell their stories as part of the healing process. Being a conduit of these truths can, at times, be overwhelming. Yet the call of the gospel is that we love one another and that we educate the world about love. When stories of shame come our way, we offer respect and love and accept them as true. This is the place where the healing takes root. Gershen Kaufman says that "shame is without parallel a sickness of the soul."[1] Individual Christians, members of faith communities, and church leaders have a crucial role to play in soul-filled healing.

This book offers both theoretical and practical grounds for the healing of this soul-sickness. The discipline of prayer, the reflections of friends and colleagues, and the depth of my passion to heal shame have made it possible for this book to reach completion. My three core values established by my faith in Jesus and lifelong commitment to the church are these: joy, abundance, and inclusion. The value of inclusion in my own faith precludes the need to define acceptable sexual behavior unequivocally. To do so would be to perpetuate sexual shame. Instead, I invite you, the reader, to take a respectfully inclusive approach to a very "hot" topic.

What Does the Bible Say about Sexual Shame?

Ancient voices of shame fill the Hebrew and New Testament Scriptures. Some of these stories will be more fully explained within the body of the book.

The ancient Hebrews shamed one another for embracing other gods, for breaking the covenant, for speaking badly about a ruler, for lack of hope in times of despair. King David danced into the city of Jerusalem with the procession of the Ark of the Covenant, only to be shamed by his wife, Micah, for exposing himself, nearly naked, to his people. Here we find a Bible story about exhibitionism! David was obviously a man of great passion, which Micah may have found quite intolerable. Did David feel ashamed when he was watching his neighbor Bathsheba bathing on the rooftop next door, or when he sent her husband to the front lines of battle to be killed so that he could have her? David had a very intense and loving relationship with Jonathan. Were they ashamed of their love? Was Micah? Certainly the saga of David illustrates the ways that passion and shame combine.

Miriam and Aaron were disgusted by their brother Moses' choice of sexual partner—the Cushite woman he chose to marry. This interracial marriage had all of the elements of sexual taboo in it. Miriam and Aaron shamed Moses because of it, and Miriam received a dose of shame in return.

We learn from many biblical stories how sexual norms are reinforced in faith communities, how personal embarrassment becomes family and community shame, and how shame is meted out differently and experienced differently by men and women. Often when two people are caught breaking the rules, the woman is the only one singled out for shame. When Miriam and Aaron criticized Moses' choice of partners, Miriam was struck down by leprosy, while Aaron was let off scot-free (Num. 12:14).

What was Ruth's experience of sexual shame when she was told to lie with Boaz so that she could inherit the property of her dead husband? Her vulnerable financial position left her no choice but to have sexual relations with Boaz to gain status, wealth, and a roof over her head.

What does the Bible tell us about sexual shame? Through the centuries women have borne the brunt of shame for the sexual assaults and incests of their fathers and brothers (2 Sam. 13:11-14). There are stories of virgins slaughtered by the foolish promises of their warrior fathers (Judg. 11:29-40) and young women turned over to visitors to be raped (Judg. 19:23-28). Was it sexual shame that caused Joseph to consider divorcing his pregnant wife, Mary? Was it sexual shame that the disciples tried to lay upon Jesus for letting a woman rub his oily feet with her hair? In the story we have called "The Woman Caught in Adultery" (John 8:1-11), we encounter Jesus' outstanding pronunciation of grace toward the woman, while the man in the scene is never even brought to the center of the crowd or exposed for his sexual behavior. We have often branded some women in the Bible as prostitutes without evidence that they were, in fact, engaged in prostitution. Is it possible that the interpreters of the Scriptures tended to project their own sexual shame into the interpretation?

These biblical stories and more will be told throughout the book as a way of looking at the pervasiveness and the damage of sexual shame to individuals, families, and congregations. As we illustrate and acknowledge the prevalence of sexual shame, its power to harm will decrease.

The story of sexual shame is rooted in ancient religious taboo and has been passed down for many generations. The dynamics of sexual shame remain the same. This book analyzes the way sexual shame operates in individuals, families, and congregations using psychological and theological perspectives. Both of these perspectives inform the perpetration of shame as well as its redemption.

Acknowledgments

I write this book in loving memory of my parents and in the healing of our family shame. My father was a gay man who lived in marriage with my mother for all of his sixty-four years. My mother chose celibacy over divorce. They both lived in the intense secret of this reality and raised me without a single word about it. I learned the truth of Dad's sexual orientation just six months before his death. Like many other people who learn that a family member is gay or lesbian, I felt that it didn't make any difference for a long while. The process of coming out of the family closet led me to do research on children of undisclosed homosexual and bisexual parents, culminating in a doctorate.

I celebrate my gay father's life. Without the love and pride of both of my parents, I would not have found antidotes for shame in my own life or been able to bring education and healing to clients and congregations.

I thank the individuals I've spoken with and the congregations who have trusted me with their experiences of shame. Their names and aspects of their stories have been changed to honor their privacy.

I thank my daughter for her influence in the writing process. This book is written so that she might know that sexuality is God's pleasurable feast for all creation and that it holds the power to praise, heal, and enliven love far beyond its power to erode, degrade, and reduce self-worth. I hope that she will learn of God's intention that we be "naked and not ashamed." She need not inherit the shame of her gay grandfather or the shame of her parents or the shame of her peers.

A few other influences led to the writing of this book. While I was pastor of a church in the San Francisco Bay Area, the following notice appeared in a counselor's newsletter: "A local writing teacher is looking for a home in which to hold a writing group." I had the available home, and teacher and author Susan Bono of Tiny Lights Publications brought the group. These women directed and fine-tuned my writing, but most importantly they challenged me to think of myself as a writer. Susan's editorial help on this book is greatly appreciated.

Thanks are also due to the women in a local group of poets and memoir writers with whom I write. They have called me to use the prophetic voice of my experience. They have inspired me by telling the secrets and the shames of their own lives, and through writing they heal themselves and me. My sincere hope is that readers of this book will find healing in its pages as well.

Introduction

I arrived at the church fresh out of seminary. My office sat on top of the fault line in the California community where I had been sent by the bishop to preach the good news. The church building had survived a few earthquakes. On my tour of the grounds, the senior pastor showed me the two-inch crack in the sidewalk that headed right through my office. A few months later I was sitting at my desk on top of that fault line when the senior pastor came to the door. He approached with an awkward shuffle, his eyes toward the floor, his head and shoulders drooping. He addressed me by name in a formal tone, sounding a bit like my father sounded when I was about to get in trouble. He stood in the door frame, looking a little shorter than his usual six feet, with one foot on each side of the fault line.

I invited him in. He didn't budge. "I just need to tell you—umm. . . . This is a little hard to talk about—umm. . . ." He was wearing embarrassment awkwardly. He had that look my mother would have called "hang dog." "Well," he said, "some people in the church think that you should wear a robe every Sunday when you're leading worship in the sanctuary." I had been wearing my robe for communion and on the Sundays that I preached, which I was taught to do in seminary. On other Sundays I wore one of my "church" dresses. This was similar to the protocol that the male pastors had been following.

"I wear my robe for communion and preaching, just like you do," I told him. We were both increasingly uncomfortable with this conversation.

"Yes, well, on the other days I wear my suit," he said, still not finding the words to talk to me about it.

"And I wear a dress, sit like a lady, and keep my knees together like my mother taught me." I had caught on to the drift of this.

"Well, some of the men have said they don't think it's right to see your legs and knees up there. You know that the choir has those privacy panels in front of them even with their robes. So I'm just asking that you wear your robe every Sunday."

1

I could feel my anger rising. I was being asked to swelter under the heat of my robe all summer long. My ordinary, bony knees were tempting someone. I had to disguise my femininity because people were uncomfortable with it. I stood up and took a step toward him, "I have the picture clearly now. They want me to cover my legs and my breasts and to wear a robe, and then maybe they can pretend there's not a woman up there."

"Well, yes, I suppose that's right . . . and I'd appreciate it if for now you could just comply. It'll take us all some time to get used to the idea of a woman in the pulpit."

Theological and Cultural Context

Here I was in my first parish, learning that worship and sexuality are to be kept strictly separate in church. Earlier I had learned about the gnostic split between the body and the spirit, a dichotomy evidently alive and well in the current day and kept intact through the use of shame as a way to establish and enforce the moral code. I was ill prepared for this incident. I had left the seminary environment and entered a disembodied body of Christ.

How do churches deal with people's bodies? What do churches say about sexuality? What do they do to provide respect for shamed individuals? How does the shame of one person affect the entire body that we call "the church"? How do congregational systems perpetuate or liberate persons from shame? These are the questions that were raised by this incident. At the time I did not have the answers and was unprepared to assess issues of sexuality in the life of the church, let alone heal them.

My gender influenced my approach to these issues and my feelings about them. The influx of women into ministry in the seventies opened the door for conversations about sexual shame. Women live an undeniable life of the flesh through monthly menstruation and childbirth. They are also more likely than men to have been sexually abused as children. They have been verbally abused by name-calling related to their genitals and sexual morality. More often than not, they have known the experience of being whistled at simply for being female.

As a woman in church leadership, I brought my female experience of being in a body that deserved respect and honor. I also brought my experience of degradation and idealization because of my body. The fact that I am a woman made this incident particularly poignant. My male colleague had not been asked to cover his body, nor was he expected to wear a skirt and expose his legs!

The theological language and training I received in seminary were imbued with the male tradition. Only two professors on our campus were women, and both taught elective courses. The shame of men around sexuality contributed to the lack of discussions of sex and the church. Since the seventies, of course, this has changed a great deal. But I have noted it again to encourage continuing discussions of sexuality in our seminaries. Church leaders need to have courses in human sexuality or sexual shame, no matter their gender or personal experience.

My first experience as a pastor came at the time of the sexual revolution, when only a few women were ordained clergy. The church was literally on a fault line, where continents (and traditions) shift. Underneath that crack through my office lay hot molten lava—sexual confusion, repression, and shame. The issues imbedded in this incident had been boiling under the surface for centuries.

Evidence of Sexual Shame in the Congregation

Both clergy and lay leaders are affected by sexual shame in the church. Many times it is felt unconsciously as a vague discomfort. A new person stepping into a church in which sexual shame is operating may feel a cloud of sadness, despite the words of the liturgy or the preaching. Sexual shame is so subtle it appears in the secrets that are kept and is spread by gossip and even prayer chains. A parishioner in describing her church to me said, "I feel like the congregation is suffering from depression." Her congregation had within its history several unspoken secrets about sexual affairs among its pastor and the laity.

Sometimes the shame is quite overt. The preacher talks about the sins of lust and infidelity, or the sermon targets gay people. The outreach committee recruits new members from married couples and fails to include single persons and older persons who are widows or widowers in events and activities. New people who come to the congregation explaining that they are "partners" or "living together" receive no follow-up invitations to events and worship. The slow-moving inclusion of women and people of color in church leadership has an element of sexual shame beneath it as well.

The congregation's request for me to robe up in the pulpit was unusually overt. It was as if Eve had stepped into the pulpit in the form of a temptress with bare knees. It was a remnant of shame from thousands of years of sexual confusion and fear, when a woman's place in life was limited by her gender to that of virgin or whore.

I was asked to "robe up" in order to quell runaway sexual impulses. Those impulses frighten us. Was I frightening those attending worship? I took some time to consider what I might have done if I were causing this discomfort. Was I unconsciously trying to seduce the congregation? Was I wearing short skirts to be flirtatious (even though it was the seventies and skirts were short)? I wrestled with my role in the situation, turned up the volume on my self-esteem meter, and went searching beyond myself to understand what was going on.

This story of congregational shame illustrates the way that shame also functions in a family system. It began with one or two individuals who felt uncomfortable about their own sexual impulses. Their concerns were communicated to the head of the family (the senior pastor) and confirmed as valid by him. Then they left it to him to enforce the family rules. The unspoken rules were redefined once someone broke them, and that person took the brunt of the consequences.

A few individuals had set the standards for everyone in an effort to protect themselves and others. The standards were enforced by codes of conduct, including issues of dress and behavior. The system used shame to reinforce these codes, and if a course correction did not follow, the individual would be in danger of being further shunned or banished.

This incident of community shaming is a classic case of "projection," the tendency of a person or a group of people to deny their own feelings and to ascribe them to someone else. I was the object of the projected sexual discomfort of some members of the congregation and possibly also the senior pastor. The anxiety response they felt within themselves was denied and disowned. They didn't sit around confessing that they were having sexual thoughts about their new pastor. Instead, they asked me to drape myself in the guise of neutered sexuality. I wasn't in a position to confront them, and, like most people who feel shamed, I internalized the "fault."

My senior colleague was, understandably, interested in gaining compliance. In an unconscious way he too had to get me "in line" or be shamed. His embarrassed posture and difficulty in making eye contact signaled to me that he was ashamed of himself. When people feel shame, they lower their eyes, and they speak in quiet whispers. He was telling a family secret that day. It was that people in church sometimes think about sex. It was that people find

women's legs erotic. Even to broach the subject with me was breaking a rule in shamed cultures: he was talking about it. In order to
quiet the critics (reinforce the norms and values of the congregation) he had to face his own shame and break the "no talk" rule that
operates in shamed systems.

I complied with the request to wear a robe. I went to the extreme.
That year my mother made three robes for me from a McCall's pattern for women's bathrobes. No one knew that I was wearing lin-
gerie! I never said or heard one further word of it in the years I
served that church family. But it would be nearly two decades
before I would ever again appear in a chancel area without my
robe. Through the heat of many summers I sweltered under my
robe while my male colleagues left their suit jackets on the chair
behind the pulpit, rolled up their sleeves, and preached the Word
with a little less heat and a little less shame.

I never forgot the small, sexy, funny, and pleasurable body that I
put under my robe the next Sunday. But in some ways that robe
was a mask. It saved me from the fear of future sexual harassment,
shunning, or complicated sexual issues. It protected me. And it
gave me a safe place from which to preach the Word in neutral,
genderless regalia.

Late in my pastoral career, I served a church that had a contemporary service one Sunday a month. On that Sunday, when everyone wore casual clothes, I kept "forgetting" and wore my robe anyway. When the elders asked me to wear casual clothes like
everyone else, I felt a sting of pain that I couldn't understand at
first. It was as if they had asked me to "disrobe." I had to go back
and relive the story of my very first pastorate and the community
that had shamed me. At first I minimized its impact. After all, it
was one small incident—but it had attached itself to other shame
feelings. In this way people who experience shame again and again
eventually become shame-bound. They lose the ability to separate
the incident from their whole identities.

How Personal Issues and Congregational Issues Interact

Since I am a child of a family that knew shame and unconsciously
passed it around, I added this incident to my spiritual and psychological self. I told myself that I'd better be careful about my
sexuality lest I face the condemnation of the community. At that
time in my life I could not have made an individual choice to go
ahead and wear whatever I wanted. Conformity meant avoiding

the shame, but it also made it impossible for me to celebrate my whole sexual and sensual self in worship. Like many church clergy and leaders, I adopted a disembodied spirituality. No matter what I was doing during the week, on Sunday I was purified and appropriately neutered.

Psychologists describe this as "splitting," a common response to shame. People who feel ashamed sexually split their "good" selves from their "bad" selves. The extreme of this is the multiple personality, the person who develops other selves so that the ones who are deeply injured by physical or sexual abuse can be, almost literally, set aside. The splitting of the person allows him or her to deny the reality of the shamed soul within.

The Mask of Shame, by Leon Wurmser, is a classic text on shame.[1] In it he describes the person who puts on a front that covers over the internal wounds of shame. If the full self is deemed unacceptable either by the remaining self or by the culture, an external self is erected. Both masking and splitting the external person provide protection against the shamed internal self.

It took many years for me to sort out my family and church-based sexual shame. At first I noticed that I was uncomfortable around some people. Later I recognized that I was like a magnet for their shame. Sometimes all I knew is that stuff just felt odd or "icky" or my stomach hurt. It took a long while to bring the issues of sexual shame into my consciousness. I still get tripped up on feelings I can't pin down. That underground lava is hot but not easy to see until it erupts.

When a little bit of shame got pushed my way at the start of my pastoral ministry, it had a tremendous impact. It took a long time to let go of that old fear and wear street clothes again at church. Before I could do that, I had to acknowledge my father's sexual shame and the shame our family reinforced. I had to fully explore my own sexuality and its complexity. I had to regain my sense of humor about the whole thing.

One hot Sunday an elderly gentleman said that he was concerned about me wearing that hot black robe in the heat, and then he asked, "What do you have on under there?" This gutsy question was met by my quick response. I blushed a little, laughed, and said, "Nothing!" Humor is a healing antidote to shame.

Fifteen years after the initial incident, I found a congregation that I trusted. It was a place where church leaders were educated about sexuality, sexual misconduct, and sexual harassment. In this setting, with casual worship the norm, I preached my first "disrobed" sermon. And I did so without shame.

1. Living on the Fault Line

This is a book about the fault line: the deep sense of unworthiness that is called "shame" and the ways that people experience it in every human relationship. Biblical texts, traditional belief and practice, and feelings of moral superiority are used to keep traditional sexual values intact. But often the messages about sexuality in the church are as vague and subtle as my first encounter with it as a pastoral leader.

Congregations today are embattled over many issues of sexuality: abortion, adolescent sexual behavior, domestic partnerships, homosexuality, clergy sexual misconduct, sex education. These areas are often reinforced by individual and social shame, though they also hold the potential to be sources of grace. Where shame is the underlying process, persons are increasingly likely to act out. When self-loathing and community shame are present, there is little room for discussion, let alone grace. When shame arises, there is a tendency to find fault.

This is not a book that's intended to fault anyone. The writing is intended to expose the *fault lines,* those places where the heat and lava threaten to destroy the church, and those places of shift that can be born with grace. With congregations in turmoil about sexuality issues, from clergy misconduct to homosexuality, we are sitting on a line no less threatening than a shifting of continental plates.

Areas of Sexual Shame in the Church Today
I recently had breakfast with one of the district superintendents of my denomination and asked him, "What is the hardest part of your job?" He paused to sip his coffee. "I think that it's dealing with homosexuality, but what takes up most of my time is clergy who have bad boundaries about their sexuality." "Oh," I said, "isn't it interesting that the church is spending all of its time on sex these days?" His reply was not atypical. "I never thought of those two issues as being the same before you said that!" Clergy and denominational leaders are often so busy looking at the crack in the walk that they can't feel the heat of the lava growing hotter just under the

9

surface. A first step in this call to healing is to invite the individual reader, the congregational study group, and the denominational leadership to look beneath the fissures and the fault lines.

All across the country clergy are taking public stands for or against the blessing of same-sex unions. When sixty-three clergy of the California/Nevada Conference of the United Methodist Church married the Conference lay leader and a long-time member of the Conference Board of Trustees in January 1999, it was viewed as a publicity event. This service joined two women, loving mothers and grandmothers who have been committed to this one faithful partnership all of their adult lives. This public action was a forerunner to a movement of great scope across the nation, where individual clergy of many denominations have made human sexuality headline news. The opening of the subject of church and state and their roles in contracts and covenants is no small earthquake. There will be many repercussions from this throughout all levels of congregational life. No congregation is untouched by what is now a public discussion of the rights and the rites of gay people. The topic has received extraordinary coverage, from talk show to small town press, but it is not the only area in which the church and sex are on people's minds.

The war rages in our congregations about whether homosexuality is a "sin" or a "blessing." Excellent resources for the study of Scripture texts regarding homosexuality are available and listed throughout this book. Congregations experience the shame that gay people feel both when they exclude them and when they shift historic positions to include gay people. The church family is in the process of coming out of the closet regarding its gay, lesbian, bisexual, and transgendered members.

Congregations are rethinking their definitions of marriage and family in light of cultural acceptance of nonmarried, long-term partnerships. Many a congregation has in its midst an elderly couple who, for reasons of financial survival, make the decision to live together and forego legal marriage. The very notion of "living in sin" is shifting.

Partly because of the rise in the divorce rate over the past twenty-five years, nearly one-third of all people in the United States today are single adults. Throughout this changing situation, the church has remained relatively silent about the sexuality of singles. Divorced persons struggle to deal with the change of sexual activity in their lives and put themselves at risk without guidance on sexual ethics from their congregations. When a fifty-year-old divorced woman goes into the drugstore to buy a box of condoms, she is aware that her religious upbringing hasn't prepared her to deal with either her embarrassment or her excitement.

James Nelson has been marking the sexual seismograph for some time. The author of many books on men's sexuality, he has been a mover in the attempt to destigmatize male sexual energy. In the 1994 Earl Lectures at Pacific School of Religion, he said that "young people are no longer willing to leave their sexuality outside the door when they enter the sanctuary."[1] When more than half of twenty-year-olds are sexually active and no one discusses sexuality and spirituality in the context of faith, young people experience the church's lack of integration and label it hypocrisy. These twenty-year-olds can't be called "dropouts" from the church; many of them have never been near one because they assume that the church will shame them for being sexually active.

Silence about male sexuality has made possible a double standard of sexual expression for women and men. But this too has been shifting. Women today have many options that allow them to engage in recreational sex, where once they were in grave danger of a procreational outcome. Biblical teachings on adultery seem old and diluted next to national coverage of a president who has multiple sexual relationships during his marriage. How many clergy condemned his morality? How many feared their own exposure as persons who had engaged in sexual misconduct? Were they silenced by their shame?

For four years I chaired a conference committee that handled issues of clergy sexual misconduct. I observed the damage of the painful repression of sexual passion that often lay underneath the acting out of sexual misconduct. When pastors violate their congregations' trust by engaging in sexual flirtation or consummation with parishioners, deep wounds result. The profile of those most likely to become sexual perpetrators of misconduct includes those who are themselves ashamed of sex. The pastor who denies his or her own strong erotic feelings is most likely to break the boundaries of relationships with others.

In the parish the pastor is expected to be God incarnate. This pressure attracts people with narcissistic tendencies and fosters narcissistic beliefs and actions. Clergy who put up a front are the ones most likely to be covering wounds to their identities at the very core of their beings. Often the wound is sexual shame. Those who feel the deepest level of personal shame are the ones most inclined to act shamefully, leaving individuals and congregations with sexual secrets and accompanying feelings of being flawed and damaged. The damage of shame leaves both the individual and the congregation with a feeling that no amount of grace and no amount of repentance or redemption can cleanse and restore them.

The shame of sexual misconduct lives in congregations for generations, just as sexual shame is passed down through families from one generation to another. If it remains a family secret, the younger generations are tempted to expose it through acting out or repeating the shameful behaviors. Not enough material has been written to help congregations heal from the sexual shame of former generations. Organizations such as the Center for the Prevention of Sexual and Domestic Violence,[2] however, have become a strong voice for education and healing around the specific sexual shame of clergy misconduct.

Why Talk about Sexual Shame?

Our silence on the subject of sexual shame has contributed to a decline in church membership. Church growth experts have been telling us for years that people drop out of the church for an average of eight years between high school and young adulthood. Perhaps we have failed to notice that these years coincide with the peak years of people's sexual activity. Many people leave the church as they come to grips with their sexual attractions. Others leave because they decide to become sexually active and don't want to be in a place where they would be morally condemned. Still others leave when church leaders are exposed as adulterers, or when clergy condemn people for their forms of sexual experimentation or expression.

When we don't talk about sexuality, we reinforce media images of it as separate from spirituality. The gap between sexuality and spirituality is a place where shame grows. Once young adults move beyond the teaching activities of a congregation, they often learn sexuality without respectful spiritual values. This increases the likelihood that they will repeat the shameful behaviors of their parents and be left bankrupt both sexually and spiritually. Without spiritual grounding for sexual relationships, young people are increasingly likely to engage in dangerous sexual practices. Sexuality and spirituality need to be taught in the same curriculum. One without the other leaves us unfulfilled.

Talking about sexuality can keep young adults in the church and open up the healing of those long burdened by a past sexual experience that has left them ashamed. A conversation about sex that focuses on respect and understanding can reverse the effects of many years of shame.

When I ask people why they have left the church, they frequently begin describing their feelings of being shunned, disrespected, ashamed, ostracized, and banished. The subtlety of covert shame leaves many to walk away wounded without any understanding of what just happened. Matthew Fox once put an advertisement in a New York newspaper, welcoming anyone who had been wounded by the church to come to a lecture. He expected fifty to a hundred people; four hundred came.[3]

My personal passion for this subject grows out of twenty years of personal observation and experience as pastor in rural, urban, and suburban congregations ranging from 96 to 420 members. Many of these congregations were shame-bound by some past experience or present exclusionary policy. Some of them were shame-bound by the very theology they taught and preached. The layers of unconscious shame blocked personal and community growth. The shame lay beneath the surface where it was covered with a crust of secrets and denials.

The Healing Begins

Hope and healing are possible once congregations and congregational leaders begin talking about the reality of sexual shame. As in family systems therapy, one healed member can begin speaking truthfully for the healing of the whole family. Individuals who have the courage are beginning to identify shame behaviors and eliminate family and congregational sexual secrets.

Am I asking that we do away with all norms and boundaries regarding sexuality? Absolutely not. The word *judgment* applies here. We need to use good judgment about our own sexuality and about the sexuality of others without shaming. When shame operates in healthy individuals, it helps us know when we are exposing ourselves too much or when we have contradicted our own value systems. When, on the other hand, shame demands that other persons' value systems be the same as ours, or when it seeks to compare their unworthiness to our righteousness, we engage in unhealthy shame. Sexual ethics based on the gospel mandate of love can shape our lives without the self-erosion that shame creates.

We therefore want to use great care before we condemn anyone's sexual desires or behaviors. Within the ethics of fidelity, mutual power, and pleasure, and based on the freedom to say yes or no to measured short- and long-term consequences, adult-to-adult activity can be given considerable latitude.

Research on sexual practices across cultures suggests a broad range of acceptable sexual behaviors—broader than ever before understood from the perspective of Euro-American immigrant people. Different cultures have different attitudes about sexual practice and about the use of shame in protecting societal norms. In my experience with Southeast Asian communities, I have found that shame takes a remarkably universal tone and serves universal purposes. Shame is used and seen as a benefit to the preservation of norms throughout societies.

Among today's many sexual problems are rising incest levels, escalating sexual exploitation of the poor around the globe, increasing teen pregnancy rates, and the AIDS epidemic. While changes have been occurring in sexual behavior, little has been done to talk about sexual ethics in light of the spiritual values of our Judeo-Christian tradition. We have allowed families to remain in their own silences about their members who are gay, lesbian, bisexual, or transgendered. Some people have left the church after deciding to live together in committed partnership without the legalities of marriage. Women who have been raped or sexually abused find little networking in the church. Teens find themselves unprepared to choose among sexual behaviors and options, and unable to fit sexuality and their religious beliefs into a cohesive and integrated whole.

Sociologist Ira Reiss has extensively researched sexual norms and practices around the world. His conclusion is that the building blocks of sexual exchange—pleasure-seeking and disclosure that build friendship and relationship—remain the same in all societies.[4] The fields of sociology and psychology have sought effectively to destigmatize sexual practices in the past twenty years. They have combined efforts through education and research to define sexual practices as diverse and to claim many previous taboos acceptable. These fields, along with a marketing of sex in the dominant culture, have kept pace with the sexual revolution of the past twenty years. But Reiss warns:

> Knowing how difficult it has been for most Americans to emotionally change their sexual ideologies . . . [we can see that] fac-

tual education alone will not be sufficient. An increased emotional acceptance of sexuality and a willingness to prepare young people for choosing to be sexually active will necessitate a change in some of our basic sexual ideologies. It is not simply a matter of learning facts. It is a matter of integrating our knowledge into a framework of values that will support different actions. This will not be easy to accomplish but the pressures of our sexual crisis in many areas moves us toward this eventuality.[5]

Most congregational leaders have come to recognize that avoidance of the subject of human sexuality has contributed to upheavals involving misconduct, abuse, moral behavior, and sexual orientation. Underneath silence about these matters lies the fear of the sexual and erotic, and underneath the fear lies the wound of shame.

John Bradshaw, author of *Healing the Shame That Binds You*,[6] has educated the public about family secrets through his many books and television programs. His work has highlighted two key points about sexual shame: (1) that it begins with rules like "don't talk about it," and (2) that many people carry issues and problems that were transferred to them from previous generations. These two work together. The more you don't talk about it, the more the secrets are passed down, producing more unspoken shame.

A simple test of the level at which sexuality is a source of shame in your church is this: Go to your church library, and look for books about sex. Look for commentaries on the Song of Solomon. Look for human sexuality curriculum for teens in your resource area. Not there?

Most churches, like families, don't do a very good job of talking with their young people about sex. The Christian perspective on sex for years has been summed up as "don't do it." Now we have a generation raised in the marketing world of "just do it," where R-rated movies include explicit sexuality. Entire book and video stores have taken up the role of advisors, trendsetters, and descriptors of the norms of contemporary society. No wonder we are being challenged to write, talk, and change our thinking about sex.

A group of adult leaders in our region were unprepared for two seventeen-year-olds who came to a weekend rally at the church. They were glued to each other's bodies for most of the weekend. When asked to sit in a large circle with one hundred other teens, these two lay on top of each other, belly to belly. The discomfort among the teens as well as the adults was palpable. I was one of the two adults assigned to bring the two youths into the office for a little chat. What we discovered was how ill prepared we were to offer these young people anything but shame. They anticipated it. "You're just so uptight about sex," they said, taking the offensive. It was difficult to argue with them about the fact that the church has in fact been uptight for a long time. We went the route of social psychologists and offered them the reality that privacy in sex keeps everyone from feeling embarrassed. We explained that embarrassment (ours and the other youths') was an indication that their love and what they did with their bodies was a private thing, not for public display.

It became clear that in a ten-minute conversation we could not instruct them on all they needed to learn about sexuality. We could not explain the sacramental nature of it or review the biblical texts about keeping their bodies as holy temples for God. We were up against a huge cultural acceptance of "all sex is okay," and their confirmed belief that the church is nothing but an uptight, old, parental moralist.

After recognizing what we couldn't do and confessing what we had failed to do, we used this incident as a starting place for the notion that we needed to include sexuality in all of our curricula and education.[7] Clearly, this was not a popular notion in our individual congregations back home, but again, those with courage can begin to move the church.

After all, we have Jesus as leader and teacher. As he went about healing, I am struck by how often the healing began with someone boldly challenging him. The woman with the flow of blood dared to touch him, and he did not condemn her, even though it made him ritually unclean. The woman begging at the gate of the rich man challenged Jesus to take notice of her. The person with schizophrenia dared Jesus to see him as a whole person. The woman at the well put Jesus to the test and then went home to convert her family and her community. The outcast and the shamed confronted Jesus and asked for his love and healing. That is what is happening today in the church.

Those whom society has shunned and abandoned are now at the doorsteps of the church with a challenge. The sexually shamed ask for our pronouncements of grace. Those whom we have labeled as unfit or unclean have showed themselves again. They have declared their own worth in the sight of God and are coming back to the church to challenge us also to declare their worth. Can we see them and accept them? We are being asked to lift the shame from ourselves and from those we have despised and rejected. We can no longer minimize the impact of sexual shame.

Where Do We Begin?

The process of healing sexual shame follows the outline of the therapeutic process for individuals and families. The first stage is the assessment of the problem. What is creating the discomfort? What has been tried to address the problem? The second stage is the diagnosis, in which an attempt is made to name the problem as this and not that. By making a diagnosis, a therapist uses her or his best judgment to say what the problem is and to begin to point toward its alleviation. The third stage is the treatment plan. What needs to take place for the person or organization to be restored? What thoughts and behaviors must shift? What beliefs must change and how will they begin to do so? What resistance is likely to emerge? The person trying to treat the individual, family, or organization looks at the whole picture and suggests a way to address the problem by enlisting them in a process of change.

Step One: The Assessment. The first chapters of this book present examples of sexual shame at work in the lives of individual Christians and their congregations. We begin now to look at the sexual-shame problems in our own congregations. What are the problems? How long have they been going on? What is the extent of the damage that has been created? Do the problems belong only to this generation, or have they been handed down from one generation to another? What has been tried in the past to deal with the problems, and how has that worked?

Readers are encouraged to hold out hope during this stage of the process, despite the pain that inevitably results from the telling and hearing of the true stories of hurt and shame. Just as in family therapy, the first stages of a client's growth happen when denial and minimization are reduced, when persons can go more deeply into the layers of defense that cover their interior feelings. When congregations peel off the outer cloak of everything being "just fine" and look at the wounds they carry, it will be painful.

Step Two: The Diagnosis. The second part of the book describes how shame works in individuals, families, and congregations. It will inform the reader about the psychology of shame in general and how to identify it in congregations. The way shame is different from guilt will be described, although the two have admittedly become "strange bedfellows" over the years.

Some of this book deals with new theory in the area of organizational psychology, and this section will walk the reader through the theory in some detail. This section follows the process a family counselor might use to help a family understand what happens in the family system when someone begins to ask for or demand change.

Step Three: The Treatment Plan. My strong conviction is that spirituality and sexuality must be integrated. This integration provides the starting place for change in the entire system of congregational life and biblical and theological teaching. The third step in the book takes the reader through the process of healing. What are the actions that laity and clergy can take to heal themselves? What are the biblical stories that can be told to proclaim grace? How can congregations articulate norms and values without using shame to reinforce them? How can congregations define and communicate the sexual norms and values that they hold? A look at the role of the congregation in healing is included in the last chapters of the book.

Questions for Reflection

1. The author lists several areas of sexual shame in congregations. What are they? Can you think of others?
2. If you are a member of a study group, why are you interested in studying sexual shame?
3. In what ways does your congregation *encourage* honest discussion about human sexuality? In what ways does your congregation *discourage* it?
4. The author includes a quote from sociologist Ira Reiss, saying, "factual education alone will not be sufficient." What kind of education about human sexuality do you feel is sufficient?
5. Does your church library contain information about human sexuality? Why or why not?
6. Why do you think that people in church don't talk more openly about human sexuality?
7. Has anyone you know been wounded by sexual shame in the church?

2. Defining Sexual Shame

Sexuality has to do with the attraction of persons for one another and the behaviors that our bodies engage in as a result of that attraction. Sexuality may or may not involve a partner; it can be expressed as feeling alive and physically playful. It may lead to orgasm, and it may not. Evelyn and James Whitehead, in *A Sense of Sexuality: Christian Love and Intimacy,* clarify the definition:

> Our sexuality includes the realm of sex—that is, our reproductive organs and our genital behavior—but encompasses much more of who we are. What our body means to us, how we understand ourselves as a woman or as a man, the ways we feel comfortable in expressing affection—these are part of our sexuality.[1]

W. C. Fields offered a more lighthearted definition when a reporter asked him, off the record, for his views on sex: "On or off the record, there may be some things better than sex, and there may be some things worse, but there's nothing exactly like it."[2]

The general use of the term *sex* has added to confusion about the topic. Sex is often used on forms to indicate gender. Individuals are not, grammatically speaking, one sex or another. They are one gender or another. In some cultures there are more than two gender options. In most of the world and in the world of the mainline church, two genders remain the norm, and these two genders have tended to be defined by God-given roles and behaviors.

Sexual identity is another commonly used term that encompasses a person's self-understanding and gender. A child develops a sexual identity at an early age, when he or she first discovers the anatomical differences between boys and girls. This is also the first stage of response to gender difference and sexual arousal. From these early experiences one develops an understanding of sexual identity, somewhat like the way one develops and explores tastes. Through experimentation and self-awareness a person grows to establish a positive, ambiguous, or negative sexual identity. This doesn't happen in a vacuum. The individual monitors his or her feelings alongside the responses and reactions of parents, family members, and peers. The developmental aspects of sexuality will be discussed throughout this book, because the greatest shaming may occur during the very vulnerable times of learning about sexuality.

With changing understandings of sexuality, the church in conflict over sexuality has not been helped by mixed information and the lack of information available from the research. Recent studies on sexual expression and the possibility that sexual orientation is genetically based make it difficult for educated Christians to maintain their former positions about sexual orientation and sin. In John 9:1-5, Jesus' disciples ask him about a man born blind: "Who sinned, this man or his parents?" If a genetic marker were found for sexual orientation, certainly Jesus' compassion would be the same as it was with the man born blind: No one's sin has caused a person to be born gay.

When Alfred Kinsey conducted research in 1948 and 1953, he found that one in ten men indicated themselves to be exclusively homosexual for at least three years of their lives; 4 percent of men and 3 percent of women in the sample were exclusively homosexual on a lifelong basis. Current research disagrees on the prevalence of homosexuality in the population, in part because no single definition has been used for research. Surveys require one to have a fixed sexual identity or attraction, a concept that is now being reconsidered among researchers.[3] Estimates are that one in four families have a homosexual or bisexual member.[4] These statistics are debatable, of course. The very private nature of sexuality and cultural norms that dictate thoughts and feelings about sexuality all influence these statistics. The debate continues about whether or not sexual orientation is a choice and whether or not we can change our sexual orientation. For these reasons, our definitions of sexuality and sexual identity need to be as clear as possible.

Sexual identity has commonly been used, of late, to indicate a consistent pattern of sexual attraction. People are attracted to those of the same gender, opposite gender, or both. For our purposes, sexual identity includes the psychological experience of being a sexual person and sharing physical and emotional intimacy. The feelings and attractions that awaken our bodies, including erotic arousal and genital response, are all considered sexual. *Sexual identity* or *orientation* will be used to indicate a person's understanding of his or her attraction as primarily homosexual, heterosexual, or bisexual.

More and more researchers are studying sexual attraction. It is likely that sexual attraction is both fluid throughout the life span and fluid across male/female attractions. Many researchers today conclude that human beings are capable of attractions to both genders and that people fall along a continuum between homosexuality and heterosexuality.[5] The days when one could declare a fixed identity are being challenged not only by the vocal presence of the gay/lesbian/bisexual/transgender communities but by scientific research with private surveys and confidential responses.[6]

What Is Shame?

There have been many excellent resources on the subject of shame[7] that take a broad look at how shame works in individuals and families. For our purposes the subject will be narrowed to sexual shame in the widening circles of the individual, family, congregation, and culture.

Finding a consistent definition of *shame* is difficult, partly because in the English language we have only one word that describes the feeling of shame in one's own eyes and shame in the eyes of others. Shame can be our own internal disappointment at not achieving our ego ideal, or it can be absorbed from family and community values. Shame takes place within the individual and also within the community.

The English term *shame* has an Indo-European base, *isikam*, meaning "hide or cover up."[8] It is often defined as the feeling of unworthiness and the tendency to avert the eyes, to hang the head. In the Garden of Eden, Adam and Eve were naked at the time of creation and unashamed. In the aftermath of the fall, they covered themselves. Shame can be understood as that feeling that creates a need to hide or cover up. Thus we have the long-standing metaphor of hiding our secrets "in the closet," a term now commonly used to describe the hiding and covering up of one's same-sex attractions and activities.

The desire to hide is sometimes evident in the posture and speech of someone who feels ashamed. Even infants have been observed to lower their heads and avert their gaze when a parent scolds them.[9] A teenaged client came to my office one day, looking toward the floor, and even though it was in the heat of summer, she wore an oversized sweater. She talked about her lost virginity and how she felt internally ashamed, wondering if I would represent the voice of the church in offering additional condemnation.

Knowing how deeply shamed she was from childhood sexual abuse, I was extremely careful to accept her sexual exploration as part of her journey toward healing and to explain it to her in this way. If a person has been shamed by a parent or community for sexual thoughts or actions, he or she will likely learn to "correct" the pleasurable thought or behavior with self-shame. Shame interrupts interest in or enjoyment of the sexual experience and replaces it with disgust, evident in the teenager's downcast eyes and blushing. The shame-bound individual may start to feel pleasure, but then the pleasure triggers a memory, and a taboo calls him or her back to the state of shame.

Individual Shame
Child development theorists believe that the experiences we have as children, seeing our own "naughty" behaviors reflected back to us in the scowling face of the parent, set the stage for our lifelong relationship with shame. If, as children, we are clear that a particular incident is a behavior we can (and actually must) change to get approval, then the feeling of shame may be corrective. A great deal of controversy rages in the psychological community and the theological community about whether shame is ever healthy. The process of helping children to develop moral consciousness and learn to self-correct based on the experience of guilt or shame is hotly debated.

I see nothing in clinical practice to indicate that chronic shame is a helpful state. While guilt motivates change, shame eats away at the core sense of well-being. And after enormous doses of shame at home or at church, individuals become shame-bound personalities. This level of affective self-condemnation can be permanently debilitating.

If most of the feedback we get from our families of origin is that not only is our behavior bad, but it springs out of a core self that is rotten or defective, then we begin to cluster negative feelings around a base of shame. If the shaming language and attitude continues to take place, people develop many adaptive behaviors to guard against feeling shame again. Distorted thoughts and patterns of self and other destructive behaviors emerge.

On the other hand, if the core self is loved and affirmed, the shame is brief and serves as motivation. As we grow older we develop the voices of the inner parent and use our own self-corrections, including shame. If we violate our own norms and values, we fall short of our own standards and experience shame.

Healthy development requires graded doses of correction that do not overwhelm the child. The developing self needs to experience respect and trust in the parent-child relationship and to have incidents of shame as minor course corrections that lead to the development of guilt and conscious choice-making. If the self is overwhelmed by shame that is experienced too intensely or too often, a shame-bound personality may develop. Kaufman notes ,that "the optimal development of conscience depends on adequate and appropriately graded doses of shame that do not overwhelm the child, but instead are effectively neutralized and counteracted. Conscience misfires because of either too little or too much shame."[10]

No one is exactly clear about the number or quality of these shame experiences that lead to shame-bound personality. Most of us end up with enough shame experiences both to correct our behavior and to keep us struggling a bit to love ourselves. I remember as a child that people used to say of someone, "He has cooties." In my town that meant that the person was someone you wouldn't want to be around because he was "gross." Maybe she smelled funny, or maybe he never looked you straight in the eye. Maybe she just seemed to take on everyone's ribbing without an ounce of self-defense. Whatever it was, I think back to those boys and girls with cooties and realize that they were the ones in shame. It became a chant with us kids when someone began to feel "icky" about themselves or others to say, "Ooh, get the cooties off." When you wrestle with your own shame, it feels a lot like that.

Adaptive Behaviors and Sexual Shame

Psychologist Mark Zaslav has described the ways in which shameful states of mind take over a person's healthy sense of self. In the shameful state of mind the individual feels him or herself to be "an exposed, vulnerable, devalued self being scrutinized and found wanting in the eyes of a devaluing other."[11] Along with the states of discomfort and extreme self-consciousness come the states of feeling "filthy or unworthy, accompanied by urges to hide or disappear."[12]

These shame-prone individuals have internalized a great deal of criticism, often because they were raised with a shaming or ashamed parent. The shame is reexperienced by these individuals when memories, fantasies, or interpersonal events trigger them. Family therapists Marilyn Mason and Merle Fossum define *shame* as "an inner sense of being completely diminished or insufficient as a person. . . . A pervasive sense of shame is the ongoing premise that one is fundamentally bad, inadequate, defective, unworthy, or not fully valid as a human being."[13]

The sexually shame-bound person has a renewed experience of shame whenever he or she feels sexual excitement or considers sexual action. Shame can also erupt as an outburst of anger. It is often masked with jealousy in the sexually ashamed person. Sometimes the shame-bound individual seeks power and control to mask the shame. This is a major contributor to sexual violence.

In healthy individuals who are raised primarily in situations of love and acceptance, shame is fleeting and corrective. If the shame is related to taboo sexual experiences in the home, church, or community, then the emotions magnify and intensify. An extremely shame-bound person cuts empathetic ties to others to protect him or herself from reexperiencing these feelings.

Gershen Kaufman combines psychodynamic theory with affect theory to understand shame, describing it this way:

> Shame is loss of face, whether at the hands of a bully or a parent [*my addition:* or God]. Shame is hanging the head, whether in response to, "You should be ashamed of yourself," or "I'm so disappointed in you." Shame feels like a wound made from the inside. Shame is dishonor, fallen pride, a broken spirit. . . . If unchecked, shame can engulf the self, immersing the individual deeper into despair.[14]

Family Shame

The shame-bound family has many ways to keep the feelings of unworthiness in place. It's not that family members consciously want to feel ashamed, but the feelings of shame keep the secrets secret. The shame keeps one bound to the family out of loyalty, by not talking about what goes on or by playing a role like the joker or the fix-it person.

In a family with many generations of unspoken incest, the shame factor keeps each generation tied to the system. A client finds herself ostracized from the family by refusing to let her children go to family events where the males who commit incest will be drinking and partying over the holidays. She faces the family dynamic that in the shame-bound system, even when she is away from the family, the blame falls on her. If she tells the truth, she is punished. She is also discouraged from getting an education or leaving the town in which these generations have perpetrated the lies of incest.

Shame enters into the dynamics of less severely traumatized families. It sets the goal of behavior and being and measures how individuals live up to or fall short of the goal. If we don't measure up to family standards, we are shamed inwardly and by the external voices of the family. Shame is accompanied by a lowering of self-esteem and an increase in feelings of unworthiness. Shame is a failure experience.

Parents who carry sexual shame transmit it to their children. This is the case with sexual shame such as incest or sexual addiction. Secrets about affairs, out-of-wedlock pregnancies, cross-dressing, or pornography use are passed down through the family. According to Kaufman, "Children of shame-based parents will inevitably activate their parent's shame, causing the cycle to repeat itself with shame passed from generation to generation."[15]

I am personally familiar with the process of family shame. As I was growing up, our family had a secret, and that secret was a source of sexual shame. My father lived the life of an ordinary family man. He went to church on Sundays with the family, he worked in administration at the university, and he kissed mom on the lips every morning on his way off to work. In all outward ways, we were a typical family. My sister and I were sweet girls who went to ballet classes after school. My mother worked at the library. No one would have suspected a thing about the shame that hung around us. My parents did not disclose the secret of my father's homosexuality or acknowledge the shame until my father's death.

As the child of a closeted gay father, I unknowingly watched what shame did to him. He was plagued with feelings of inadequacy, and he was secretly bitter that he was not like everyone else. For years he tried to be someone different for my mother's sake and for the sake of the family. He tried his mightiest to live as a heterosexual man. Although these feelings were rooted in the ignorance of the culture and the church in which he worshiped, he took them into himself, and they nagged him with a constant lowering of his self-esteem. He was painfully aware that he could not live a full life with honesty because of the shunning of the culture. The shame of his own failure to be "normal" was overwhelming and intense. Growing up around it, I inherited an unconscious dose of that shame. It was like breathing in secondhand smoke at home with my family.

How is shame transmitted? Shame is passed down from one generation to another. Psychologists talk about scenes of shame that get stuck in the memory of the child.

Shame-based syndromes that develop within individuals cause shame-based family systems to form. There is, however, a critical intervening step in the development of such syndromes and systems. Parental shame is embedding in a series of governing scenes. It is these original childhood scenes of the parents that later become reactivated by their own children. Like magnets, scenes compel reenactment. Phenomenologically, a scene is an entrance, a psychological "black hole" drawing the conscious adult self inward. It is a portal in time. The mature self is immediately transported back into these original scenes, which then are re-experienced fully. Once a governing scene has been reactivated the original experience is relived in the present with all its affect (feeling) reawakened.[16]

In Christian families these scenes are often related to church life and faith. I remember the atmosphere that overtook our family living room when my father's brother brought over tracts to remind us that playing cards and going to dance club was "sinning." These tracts no doubt also listed sexual sins about which my father likely experienced shame. On the day of my father's funeral, this same relative walked up to the pastor and said, "Well, I guess we'll never know if he made it into heaven or not." The shame of this comment is seared into my heart and related to the shame my father felt about being gay. His brother didn't even know that Dad was gay; he simply doubted God's acceptance of a man who played bridge and went to dance club.

A word from the pulpit, a sideways glance at church, a song or hymn about unworthiness—these all serve as governing scenes for shame in Christian individuals and families.

Cultural Shame

Some languages have more than one word for shame; one word denotes internal personal shame, while the other denotes the shame of the community toward an individual or group. In English we lack the words to separate the feeling of being exposed to the self as unacceptable and the feeling of being shunned or disbarred from the community. Both feelings, however, are operative within the church. Persons come to the church loaded down, seeking a lifting of their unworthiness.

Henri Nouwen, priest and author, tells about his work with children and adults with mental disabilities. As he was preaching one morning in the chapel at a residential facility, a little girl with Down's syndrome came and stood directly below the pulpit, looked up at him, and said, "Henri, I want you to give me a blessing. Henri, I need a blessing, Henri." Henri looked down and said, "I'm preaching right now. I'll give you a blessing after the service." The little girl sat down but got up again in a few minutes. She walked forward and stood directly beneath him. "Henri, I need a blessing, now, Henri." Again he told her that he would finish the service and then offer her a blessing.

Keeping his word, after the worship service had ended, Henri called the little girl to come forward and stand before him. Taking her face in his hands, he said, "Susan, you are God's beloved child. God loves you and blesses you and cares for you always." And as he looked up from her face, he was startled to see that a line had formed behind her; everyone in the church was waiting to be blessed, to be loved, as well.[17]

This wonderful story illustrates the power of blessing as an antidote to feelings of unworthiness. The little girl's urgency was no less than our own. If we feel internally flawed, the cure sought may be a sense that God has accepted us just as we are. We call this gift "grace." The blessing is the individual cure.

If one feels shamed in the family, it's the family or a family of choice that undoes the power of the wounding. If one is wounded by the community, one needs acceptance and reconciliation within community. The blessing of the elder, priest, rabbi, or minister is the blessing that cures the shaming of the community. When one feels shamed by the community of faith, it sinks in deeply and becomes personal. Kaufman notes, "To live with shame is to feel alienated and defeated, never quite good enough to belong. And secretly the self feels to blame; the deficiency lies within."[18]

Communities and cultures use shame to keep people in line, to protect the traditions of the culture, and to keep religious laws sacred. Shame is directed toward minority groups or individuals who violate the rules. And the individual may be guilty of no crime other than violation of the "norms" of the culture or the church.

Internal feelings of unworthiness may result entirely from the external community and its values. This is often the case for gay, lesbian, bisexual, and transgendered people. The term "internalized homophobia" describes the way in which people absorb the sexual shame of the community and place it upon themselves. In many people who are angry and hostile toward gay people lies an underlying experience of personal sexual shame. Zaslav calls this the "attack-other mode" of defense against feeling one's own shame. The other is put down in order to adjust the balance of power between self and other. This dynamic is also at work within abusive relationships. In chapter 10, in the discussion of rules of the shame-bound system, I describe some people in churches who live with shame that has been turned into the "attack-other" mode.

While we are all vulnerable to feeling shame or being ashamed in the presence of others, to be sexually shamed is often the most difficult wound to heal. If you are ashamed of your gender, your sexual activity, your sexual abuse of someone, or sexual abuse of which you were the victim, or if you are ashamed of your sexual attractions, partner choices, and activities, huge areas of the self are overwhelmed. One of my university professors said that he had read that men think about sex once every thirty seconds and women think about sex once every minute and a half. If you feel ashamed of yourself every time a thought on sex comes up, it will cloud your entire way of being in the world.

Who are you when you look in the mirror? Who are you when you communicate with a friend, a lover? Who are you when you are all alone experiencing arousal? Who are you when you sing "Amazing Grace" in church? Are you more aware of your wretchedness or your salvation? If you dig down deeply into your soul, do you like what you see? Can you believe in your own worth? If you can't, you may be carrying sexual shame. In the presence of God, you may feel that your body or your spirit is condemned.

Too often the search for grace and redemption goes on in silence. People don't feel safe enough in their congregations to talk about their self-loathing. Feeling ashamed of their sexual lives—past, present, or imagined future—people act out their despair under the guise of different issues in congregations. Hoping for grace, hoping for the blessing, the shamed too often find their self-condemnation reinforced. God's perceived condemnation deepens the unworthiness and presents a further roadblock to healing.

How Shame and Guilt Interact

Confusion frequently arises about the difference between guilt and shame. They are not the same. Guilt is the conscience telling us that we have done something wrong. It serves as a protection for us, as a warning sign that we have violated our own values. With guilt we have injured others or ourselves by a behavior that is unacceptable. The action is judged wrong (either internally or externally) and must be amended. If we go through a process of confession, forgiveness, and restoration, the guilt is relieved.

With shame, actions are not the whole story. Our very beings are at fault. It isn't simply that I hurt my brother, but that I am not worthy of my brother's forgiveness. When the prodigal son returned to his father's house, the father had forgiven him for his actions. The young man said to him, "I'm no longer worthy to be called your son, treat me like one of your hired servants" (Luke 15:19). The father's treatment of him as royalty was the cure for his shame. He told the boy, in actions louder than words, that no matter what his actions had been—the throwing away of the inheritance, the "dissolute living" (Luke 19:13; a sexual matter?)—he needn't hang his head in shame. He was accepted, restored, and honored.

People who are shame-bound don't have the ability to separate their guilt about unjust or unkind actions from shame about unworthiness made evident by shameful actions. If you've ever tried to tell a shame-bound person that his or her behavior was unacceptable to you, you've felt the difference right away. The shame-bound person won't be able to see the action as the issue. He or she will feel condemned to the core by your very mention of any mistake. This deflects the conversation away from the guilt-producing behavior and reinforces the shame.

The blurred distinction between guilt and shame is especially true in sexual shame. The person who has a one-night stand and begins to feel bad afterward doesn't usually use those feelings to go through a process of confession and forgiveness. What is more often felt is shame, that the behavior destroyed the person's worth or integrity. Guilt is a matter of legality, of a broken contract, so that if the person were married, he or she would likely endure the guilt of breaking a covenant. And underneath the guilt would grow a cesspool of ill feelings toward oneself. This growing sense of disgust with oneself is known as shame. While the guilt may find forgiveness and release, it is much harder to replace the self-esteem lost to self-betrayal.

Further Notes on Sexual Shame

In some cases the shame belongs to actions—sins of either omission or commission. In other cases the shame is the result of a violation of the person's character. Sexual shame, which so often arises from sexual assault, incest, rape, or other violence, deeply wounds the person and blurs the normally healthy distinction between actions and character deficits.

Sexual shame is the emotional experience of unworthiness that clusters around events from the past. It involves those aspects of human sexuality that are generally not changeable—attraction and gender. As I explained in the introduction, my being a female in the chancel area wasn't something I could do anything about. What could be done was the covering up of my body so that it would not tempt others. In that instance I was being asked to take responsibility for other people's denied sexual feelings. The shame happened about my unchangeable gender and was an attempt to nullify the transient feelings of anxiety in those who observed it. This instance also illustrates the way that tradition plays a part in sexual shame. Choir members had been covered from the waist down with privacy panels for years. The shame was imbedded in the tradition itself.

Here are some of the unchangeable sexual concerns that are not discussed in most congregations: sexual attraction, feelings of sexual arousal, prior sexual experiences, reproductive education, menstruation, menopause, and sexuality at different life stages. An even longer list of unspoken sexual concerns includes those sexual behaviors that have some element of change and choice in them: choices in sexual partners, sexual pleasure, masturbation, pregnancy, experimentation, and impotence. Lastly, we rarely address a group of topics on human sexuality that potentially create hard-to-heal psychological shame: sexual addictions, sexual violence, sexual deviations, sexual harassment, sexual coercion, prostitution, and the use of pornography.

Sexual Shame Syndromes

A thirty-year-old male was sent to a therapist with a diagnosis of sexual compulsion. The man struggled, he said, with a desire for multiple sexual partners, and he had frequent sexual relationships prior to his marriage. His Christian background and, even more significant, his wife's conservative beliefs led to greater intensity in his feelings of shame about this, even though he had been faithful to her for the seven years of their marriage. When she was diagnosed with fibroid tumors, it became impossible for them to have intercourse. His entire sexual libido became focused on his "shame-filled thoughts." His manhood was challenged. He went through what he called "a time of temptation."

Therapy included an exploration of the couple's sexual pleasures. These people had never been given permission to experiment with varieties of sexual pleasures within marriage. They did not know that sexual pleasure could take place between them without intercourse. The church prohibitions about masturbation had extended into the couple's relationship and limited their choice-making around sexual pleasure. The therapy redirected the man's sexual urges within the relationship. He began to address his shame-based feelings about sex formed early in childhood and in his family where many sexual secrets were operative. His course of treatment illustrates the way that shame limits sexual options, closes down discussion between partners, and serves to deny an individual of pleasure. Sometimes this shame is short-lived, but more often than not it is the result of clusters of feelings reinforced at home and in church.

According to affect theory,[19] the organizing scenes of shame that connect together in the shame-prone individual may form large enough groups of thoughts and feelings to be called *syndromes*. Several sexual shame syndromes are believed to exist. The first is a group of affective disorders known as sexual compulsions. These disorders reproduce shame so that the feeling of shame can be reduced or overcome. The focus of the behavior is an attempt *not* to feel shame this time. These compulsions may be repeated sexual partnerships with no regard for the content or longevity of the relationship, exhibitionism, sexual fantasy, pornography use, or excessive masturbation—any behavior that decreases healthy functioning in a primary relationship. When feeling shame about these behaviors, the compulsion is actually an attempt to rid oneself of the disgust or *dismell* (a term used by Silvan Tomkins to describe an odor that is distasteful to the point of repulsion). Persons who engage in compulsions like these are seeking the power of them to numb or sedate the negative feelings associated with shame. If the sedative effect works, they will repeat the behavior. When the feeling of shame becomes overwhelming, the behavior that numbs that feeling will become the person's first priority.

Sexual abuse is another class of compulsive syndromes. Centered in violence and the need to control another to rid oneself of intense feelings of powerlessness, sexual abuse leaves the perpetrator and victim alike with crippling shame. Kaufman writes:

> Incest and rape are two distinct types of sexual abuse that activate intense inner states of powerlessness, bodily violation, and humiliation. In the midst of shame, one feels to blame. Childhood incest generates poignant, often crippling shame. . . . When the experience of violation, helplessness, and betrayal is disowned, the self withdraws deeper inside to escape the agony of exposure.[20]

Sexual abuse scars both the victim and the perpetrator. As they keep the secret of the assault, the two may become even more enmeshed emotionally. They have a shame-based relationship. The victim becomes the perpetrator in the desperate attempt to recast the roles and regain emotional and physical power. In situations of incest, the child victim may become a willing or even seductive participant in order to try to normalize the horror of the experience. The shame this creates is deep and long lasting. Adults who were victims of incest may pick a partner who will later molest their children. These persons are "scripted" by the scenes of shame that first affected them. In all cases intense humiliation is the dominant feeling. Without healing interventions, the scenes of these violations of self are stored in the memory and reenacted or split off and disowned.

Tomkins has done a great deal of work on sexual addiction as a way to deactivate a suppressed feeling.[21] Those who normally avoid emotional responses, suppressing or repressing their own feelings, may seek sexual involvement with indiscriminate partners in order to feel their own intense feelings. The person who is trying to minimize his or her negative feelings about sexuality may engage in intense levels of sexual activity in order to override these feelings with positive affect. The rekindling of sexual excitement overwhelms the feeling of sexual shame. Kaufman writes:

> Thrills must be sought continually, and when the object no longer provides them, the incessant quest after excitement is renewed. When excitement promiscuity enters the sexual sphere of life, the individual is forced into sexual promiscuity in search for excitement. The endless striving for affect payoff overshadows even strong ties of enjoyment in more enduring love relationships. The quest after excitement dominates the personality.[22]

The cycle goes like this: A shamed person goes in search of a way to lessen the feeling of humiliation. One way to do this is to escape from it by finding ways to numb the pain; this may take the form of sexual addiction. The compulsive behavior reduces the initial feeling of shame, but it also reproduces it and the cycle starts all over again.

Sexual dysfunction is often the result of a shame-based past experienced emotionally in the present. Sexuality requires the joining together of pleasure, safety, positive feelings, a boost of self-esteem, the experience of power, and potency. The sexual drive relies on good feelings to move it along. If memory and schema (the scenes of life) connect the sexual drive to sexual abuse, the natural flow of positive feelings is interrupted. A woman who is recovering from a childhood rape finds her sexual interest in her husband interrupted by the touch of his cheek on hers when he has a growth of beard. The scratch triggers all of her emotional memory of the disgust of the assault. She cannot will herself to continue. She must back up and start again with her husband freshly shaven.

Sexual impotence in men and anorgasmia in women are often the secondary experiences of sexual shame. The fear of being "seen" or "exposed" is often at the core of the problem. If you had, as a young client of mine had, the experience of your stepfather asking you to take off your clothes in front of him so that he could look at you, you would carry shame about being seen. You might develop an aversion to any sexual exchange that involved someone looking at you. Your lack of sexual availability to your partner would further shame you.

When those who experience impotence find themselves humiliated, shame increases. For those who feel sexually inadequate or have premature ejaculation or a lack of orgasm, shame grows even greater. The cycle of shame-begets-shame continues. The feeling of shame joins together with humiliation, powerlessness, anger, and disgust with oneself, or projected onto the other. In people with normal character development, these feelings can create compulsive, harmful, sexual behaviors. To label them "sin" or to condemn these people outright as a group using lists of biblical "sinners" would be to reinforce their behaviors. While boundaries must be set for loving sexual behavior, the healing must be handled with extreme care that shame not be increased.

Additional syndromes deserve mention at this time. The characterological disorders of narcissism, borderline personality, and the schizoid personality are all potentially sexually shame-based identities. In narcissism, the sexually shamed individual creates a pretend exterior self to compensate for the inner core of worthlessness. This syndrome has been referred to earlier in the book and will be extensively reviewed in a subsequent chapter. The narcissistic syndrome is of particular interest to congregational leaders because many clergy have some level of narcissistic character and because the church fosters narcissism in clergy.

The borderline individual may also be a product of a shame syndrome. The borderline, like the narcissist, attempts to split off the good self from the shamed self. The borderline's childhood was filled with volatile and untrustworthy parenting. In response the borderline longs to be loved but pushes love away with rage. This person is desperate for love and at the same lacks trust in it. The schizoid personality has split off from self and society. This disorder is characterized by a total fear of intimacy, closely guarded by detachment. The individual with multiple personality disorder has created multiple selves in order to cope with an intensely shamed inner core. People who were repeatedly sexually abused as young children develop additional personalities in order to protect themselves during the trauma. Beneath the many personalities lies a core shamed self.

A last group of shame-based people is believed to have no moral consciousness. The syndromes listed previously were coping mechanisms for shame by shifting the feeling around, splitting it off, overwhelming it with positive feelings, letting it attach to rage or withdrawal. A last group of shame-bound people behave "as if" without shame. Psychopathic individuals never bonded with a parent and never experienced love and the closeness of a relationship. They therefore never developed a capacity for empathy—the ability to understand another's feelings. The psychopath or the antisocial personality experiences shame in the presence of others but has no internal development of it. No conscious correction of shameful behavior has been developed. This is what makes these individuals dangerous to themselves and others.

We might each presume that "my congregation doesn't have persons with sexual shame syndromes." But this would be false. Many of the problems we have discussed have so much shame attached to them that they are deeply hidden and covered up. Even the thought of conversations about them might make some individuals very uneasy. This fact draws people with these issues into the congregation, rather than limiting their participation. If a church turns its view away from all things sexual, it becomes a haven for those with deep sexual wounds and for those who act out sexually through abuse, addiction, or repression. The shame that goes looking for a safe hiding place may find it in a congregation near you.

Questions for Reflection

1. How are sex and sexuality the same or different?
2. Do you think that sexual orientation is fixed or fluid? Why?
3. The author suggests that "closets" hide and cover up sexual attractions and activities. What closets exist in your congregation?

4. Is shame ever good for you?
5. Are shame and moral conscience the same or different?
6. Do you know any shame-prone people?
7. Is anyone in your family the one who shames others?
8. How are shame and guilt different or the same?
9. Does anyone in your congregation use Zaslav's "attack-other" mode to get rid of his or her own shame?
10. Congregations may attract people with sexual addictions. Do you agree or disagree with that statement? Why?

3. Major Shifts in the Study of Human Sexuality

Sexuality Research

Alfred C. Kinsey conducted the most prominent and culture-shaking research on human sexuality back in 1948.[1] My father, a master's level student in psychology, had a copy of Kinsey's work in his study. By the time I was a curious teen, looking for information on sexuality, this book looked as old and interesting as my grandmother's German Bible. I didn't know the language of either text. Kinsey's book was a compilation of statistics that I could not interpret and seemed to be unusually focused on men. At the time, I had no idea that my father was doubting his own sexual orientation; I only knew that we had a huge book on men and sex in the house, and it didn't give an adolescent girl anything she wanted to know!

I had no idea of the revolutionary nature of the Kinsey text. He conducted the most detailed and comprehensive survey on human sexuality in the history of humanity, opening the door for candid reporting about human sexual attraction and activity. His two books, *Sexual Behavior in the Human Male* (1948) and *Sexual Behavior in the Human Female* (1953), detailed precisely the activities of adults, including numbers and choices of partners, and the frequency of their sexual activities. As a behavioral scientist, Kinsey published volumes that reshaped American thinking about human sexuality.

Kinsey was not the first to study sexuality. Nearly 5,000 years ago the Yellow Emperor in China was interested in learning more about how to please the women in his life. He conducted a survey for a book on sex titled *Secret Instructions Concerning the Jade Chamber*.[2]

Just prior to Kinsey, however, a lesser-known researcher studied the sexual attitudes of women. Helena Wright, a gynecologist who worked in London at a clinic for the poor, was curious about the actual sexual practices of working-class women. She found most of the women of this era to be misinformed, dissatisfied, and ashamed to discuss the topic. She was the first woman to publish information for couples about the sexual anatomy of women and the arousal cycle. Convinced that the texts would be banned upon publication, Helena and her publisher buried copies of the first printing.

These researchers boldly mined the underground layers of people's true sexual needs and practices, despite the layers of social and religious conditioning that had taught the world to keep these matters private. These researchers made the false assumption that sexual privacy protects against feelings of exposure and shame. The actual effect of intense privacy for all things sexual has been to use sexual shame as a form of social control. Dominant sexual practice could be deemed the "norm" and all else rejected. If we are ignorant about our true differences, we can presume to know the one and only theologically and historically valid perspective. While the church has long said that sexuality is a private matter, it has been successful in keeping all variations in sexual practice out of mainstream belief and education. This has helped to define the norm of sexual practice within the bedroom of two married persons, one male and one female.

Procreation Only

For centuries the Roman Catholic Church and many of its children among Protestant denominations have held a "procreation only" position. While sexuality for its own sake has been decried from the pulpits of Catholic and Protestant churches alike, an exception to its sinfulness is made for the purposes of procreation. Across the years of sexual history, procreation-only sex has maintained male power. It has ensured property rights and the maintenance of control of women and children for economic stability. The old tradition of the bride being passed from the father to the groom is yet a symbol from this not-long-forgotten time.

The church has not shed its insistence that sex is tolerable only as biological necessity. This has been challenged in the past century by psychological and sexual behavior research. Researchers have found that people engage in sexuality for many reasons, among them desire to connect through knowing and being known and the simple search for pleasure. While exploitative sexual practices and addictions create deep level of sexual shame, the church's silence on these matters hasn't provided education for healthier choices.

Rather than throw its influence into an educational role about sexual ethics and sexual spirituality, the church has become a combatant in the fight for the "norm" of sexually rigid roles. While the past twenty years have produced a revolution in sexual knowledge and education, the church has been silent in the face of its own sexual shame. Moreover, the chasm between spirituality and sexuality has been widening.

The Church in an Age of Sexual Awakening

By the 1970s the church in the United States found itself in an age of sexual awakening. The invention and availability of the birth control pill opened sexual freedom for many women. The increased availability of abortion equalized the consequences of adult sexual behavior across class, race, and gender lines. Kinsey's report was followed by Shere Hite's surveys on sexuality in the 1980s, redefining American culture's views on prevailing sexual practices. The media quickly grabbed up increasing numbers of statistical reports that showed sexual activity at greater rates and variations than previously reported. The marketing world sold products through sex, and the television and movie worlds became transfixed by sexuality. Where was the voice of the church in the midst of this change?

Concepts of sexual behavior are in cultural flux. Norms and standards are constantly changing. The law once prohibited physicians from informing women of the nature of how pregnancy takes place, even when the women's lives were at risk from further pregnancies. Today nearly every woman in the country has access to contraception. This shift moved sexuality beyond the property and procreation venues and started a liberation of female sexuality. Separating procreational sex and recreational sex opened the way for greater cultural acceptance of homosexual and bisexual practice.

How far have we come from the Yellow Emperor's book? We have learned a great deal about sexual expression and about physiological sexuality. We have seen sexuality move from the dark of the bedroom into the light of dinner conversation. We have observed the politics of sexuality and the oppression and repression of it.

Despite the entire acceptance of sexual behavior and the research about it, we cannot help being concerned about generations of youths who are sexually active at younger and younger ages. Teenagers are exposed to sexuality and sexual behaviors at increasingly younger ages. At a local high school in a nearby community, the slide show for the day's family health class was on sexually transmitted diseases, including pictures of genital warts. When I arrived at a local church as the new pastor in the 90s, I asked one of the youths what they do at youth group. "Oh," she said, with a giggle and a blush, "we just sit around and talk about sex." At last, I thought, I had arrived at a church where sexual shame was lifting. As it turns out, the leader offered no guidance at all, except to talk about his new live-in girlfriend. No ethics discussions, no conversation about the values and emotions involved, no reading of Scripture. The era of sexual openness has caught the church ill prepared for these discussions.

Questions for Reflection
1. Research on human sexuality is hard to obtain. How accurate do you think it is?
2. What influences the attitudes that people have about sexuality in your culture?
3. What level of influence do you think the church has over people's sexual choices?
4. What type of and amount of sexual education do you feel is appropriate in your church/synagogue? In your schools? In your homes?
5. What values and norms about sexuality have changed during your lifetime?
6. Do you consider these changes healthy?

4. Judeo-Christian Sexuality

The Purity Codes

I went to church every Sunday during those years of cultural, sexual change. I never heard one word about sex. In 1975, when I was planning my wedding, my father joked that instead of saying, "her mother and I do," he was going to say, "be fruitful and multiply." This was the sum total of my sexual preparation for marriage. Be fruitful and multiply. No little book on how to do it, not one statement about the pleasure of it. Just the facts.

My parents abided by the rules of their Victorian ancestors. Women's role was to be the empty vessel, and women were not expected to experience sexual pleasure. The goal was procreation. All other aspects of sexuality were considered sinful. The ghosts of this perspective still haunt us.

Judeo-Christian teachings about sex have their roots in the purity laws of the Hebrew Scriptures. A historic overview of these laws, which are regulations dealing with human sexual activity and ethics, can be found in William Countryman's *Dirt, Greed, and Sex*.[1] His thorough review of Hebrew Scriptures and the Christian texts reveals the alien worlds of sexual ethics in the biblical era and today. He draws a set of ethical principles relating to sexuality and purity laws from the Scriptures.

Countryman advances the cause of creating biblical and ethical guidance for Christians. He notes:

> The creation of its own purity code has been one of several ways in which the church has at times allowed itself to become a barrier to the gospel of God's grace. A Christian sexual ethic that remains true to its New Testament roots will have to discard its insistence on physical purity. . . . To be specific, the gospel allows no rule against the following, in and of themselves: masturbation, non-vaginal heterosexual intercourse, bestiality, polygamy, homosexual acts, or erotic art and literature. The Christian is free to be repelled by any or all of these and may continue to practice her or his own purity code in relation to them.[2]

Countryman also says that sexual education is ignored due to the anxiety Christian teachers and role models feel about sex. He concludes that the modern consequence of the old purity laws includes teenage pregnancy, the rise and spread of AIDS, and the dilemma of children raising children.[3]

The church has consistently linked sexuality with sin. Categories of sins are delineated in Scripture, yet many are overlooked and ignored. Failure to feed the poor is cited as "sin" more often than fornication and sodomy. Robert Albers, in *Shame: A Faith Perspective*, writes:

> In the hierarchy of sins that has been constructed by the church . . . the sins associated with the body seem to receive the most attention, whether it be lust, fornication, or adultery. The persistent sins of the spirit such as envy, jealousy, slander, hatred, and judgmentalism, which slay the spirit within others, are often ignored. This negative emphasis is the genesis for much shame associated with the body and its functions.[4]

Early Christian Teaching

For much of its history, Christianity has emphasized a strong separation of body and spirit, leading some to consider the body "bad" and the spirit "good," thereby reinforcing our modern-day lack of clarity about sexuality. In the first century Paul advocated celibacy, if at all possible, as the best way to give oneself fully to the service of Christ. This set the stage for the shaming of those who couldn't measure up to the ideal. In 386 CE Pope Siricius attempted to forbid church elders to make love with their wives. Scholar Reay Tannahill describes the early church fathers as linking sex and sin. She writes: "It was Augustine who epitomized a general feeling among the church fathers that the act of intercourse was fundamentally disgusting. . . . Arnobius called it filthy and degrading, Methodius unseemly, Jerome unclean, Tertullian shameful, Ambrose defilement."[5] A closer look at these church fathers might reveal their own preoccupations with sexuality as stemming from interpersonal or intrapersonal shame.

Augustine, whose writing shaped Catholicism's views on sexuality for seven hundred years, was himself troubled by desires and temptations he could not control. According to Evelyn and James Whitehead, "Augustine remembers his youth as a season of obsession in which he hungered for respect and esteem (6:6). He clung compulsively to his friends (4:6); he was constantly swept away by the impulses of his sexual appetite."[6] Augustine lived in a common-law relationship with a woman who satisfied his sexual needs but was not the respected woman his mother sought for him in marriage. His pain at leaving the woman he had been with was intense, and since his arranged bride was too young to marry, he was forced to wait two years for her. His passion was too great, and he took a mistress. With shame he admits his sinfulness: "In the meantime my sins were multiplied. . . . I was not so much a lover of marriage as a slave of lust, so I procured another woman, but not, of course, a wife" (6:16). In the midst of this frustrated mixture of sexual desire and longing for love, Augustine's confusion was overwhelming. Could this have been his reason for fleeing to the church and embracing a celibate life? Theologian Margaret Miles surmises: "We must accept Augustine's evaluation of himself as addicted to sex, from which, he tells us, no friendship was free." He himself described his life as "tormented."[7]

What degree of sexual shame drove him to the cloister? Psychology would tell us that Augustine's shame, like that of many of the church patriarchs, was projected onto the congregations with an inflated fervor. The need to rid the world of sexual sin was preached by those who had a powerful internal sense of sin and failure in the sight of God. Thousands of years of European church history reflect the confused and tempted feelings of men fighting their own sexual impulses.

A fear of the flesh and denial of sexual impulses have left us with a disembodied theology and a great deal of shame and self-loathing. History reveals the deep chasms that have characterized spirituality and sexuality in Christianity. Sam Keen, in *The Passionate Life*, writes:

> Romance did not thrive in the atmosphere of Christian theology. Much of the sexual ethic of western Christendom was tainted by the Gnostic-Manichean dualism that regarded matter as degraded, nature as the creation of a demonic god, women as inferiors, and sex as lust to be repressed or expressed only within marriage. Had Augustine not felt so guilty for loving his mistress, the Middle Ages might have recognized that sexual feelings were one of the delightful gifts of the Creator. As it was, Christianity fell into an anti-erotic posture; glorifying virginity, degrading women, linking sex to guilt, discouraging romance, denying the flesh, casting suspicion upon sensuality.[8]

Christians in Search of Sexual Freedom

Those who first sought religious freedom in America were no less obsessed with the subject of sexual sin. Though they fled religious persecution, sexual sin remained an area with absolutely no freedom. The witch-hunts were directly linked to the fear of women and women's sexuality. In the late nineteenth century people were brought up on morality charges, and Congress passed the Comstock Laws, which forbade certain sexual practices. Within the past decade, attempts have been made to strike down the last of the "sodomy laws" from state statutes. According to the American Civil Liberties Union (ACLU), eighteen states and Puerto Rico currently have sodomy laws.[9] James Haught comments: "Western religions have spent millennia inflicting shame, guilt, repression, and punishment upon human sexuality."[10] In an effort to preserve traditional families and to limit sexual deviance, Christians have too often turned against members of their own families and members of their congregations.

In the past twenty-five years, rapidly changing cultural shifts in attitude and practice regarding sexuality have left the church vulnerable to the kind of messages the media spreads. The lumbering giant of an institution that we call "the church" has taken a great deal of time to change. It is at the heart of the tension between the preservation of the morality of the past and shifting cultural norms and practices.

Will today's church be as fervent a leader in the fight for sexual justice as it has been for other justice movements? Certainly its long history of sexual repression and shame may make this difficult. Congregations who felt passionate about justice produced the leaders of civil rights movements at home and abroad; it is the passion of congregations that opened the door to women in ministry. The church has worked for justice throughout the centuries. In the area of sexuality, however, we find that the issues become personal so quickly and become so shame-bound from years of silence that the movement toward justice moves slowly.

The tension is rising and becoming increasingly evident. A September 24, 1999, article in *The Charleston Gazette* by Rev. Randy Wilson, pastor of Esta Memorial Baptist Church, voiced his opposition to proposed state legislation that would expand the protection of human rights and hate crime laws to include gay men and lesbians. He wrote, "This law would be one more step down the road to making criminals of the God-fearing people of Kanawha County who have enough intestinal fortitude to speak against sodomy. It would put the righteous in jail, while leaving the Sodomite to prey on the unsuspecting youth of our society. . . . All of their talk, all of their crying, all of their arguments are nothing more than a smoke screen to cover for them, while they weasel their way into our society as normal people. They are not normal people. Romans Chapter 1 says they are reprobate people. They are not fit for society and should be put in jail." The *Gazette*'s editor responded: "His essay sounds rather like the way Nazis once spoke of Jews, treating them as loathsome inferiors unfit for human society. . . . For a minister to hate a small group of people just because biology made them different from him is sadly depressing."[11]

The church has been attempting through legislation to resolve these tensions. The Presbyterian Church U.S.A. in June 1999 reaffirmed its position against the ordination of gay, lesbian, bisexual, and transgender leaders, both clergy and laity. The United Methodist Church is in an uproar regarding the celebration of holy union services, seen as the sanctification of homosexuality. Yet *The United Methodist Book of Discipline* states:

> We recognize that human sexuality is God's good gift to all persons. We believe persons may be fully human only when that gift is acknowledged and affirmed by themselves, the church and society. We call all persons to the disciplines, responsible fulfillment of themselves, others, and society in the stewardship of this gift. We also recognize our limited understanding of this complex gift and encourage the medical, theological, and social science disciplines to combine in a determined effort to understand human sexuality more completely. We call the church to take the leadership role in bringing together these disciplines to address this most complex issue.[12]

This statement in itself admits to the confusion in the church and culture about the goodness and danger of sex. Alongside this statement, the *Book of Discipline* forbids the conducting of services of "holy union" by its clergy or in its churches.

Recently the United Methodist Church's General Board of Church and Society supported the New Jersey Supreme Court's ruling in the case of *James Dale v. the Boy Scouts of America* in strongly condemning discrimination based on sexual orientation. The United Methodist men's organization took a stance in support of the Boy Scouts of America. A United Church of Christ in northern

California was turned down when they requested the founding of a new Boy Scout Troop. The church's standing as an "open and affirming" congregation influenced the area leaders to deny their request. The inner and outer turmoil of these debates leaves very little educational opportunities for young people to explore the scriptural and spiritual aspects of human sexuality. Church leaders surely realize that the taboo forbidding all open discussion of human sexuality leaves Christian teachings on sex in shambles—mixed with superstition and prejudice and adhering to no set of coherent ethical or political principles.

In the past fifty years significant sexual justice movements have taken place. Women have claimed their right to contraception and abortion. Gay, lesbian, bisexual, and transgendered people have demanded their rights to fair housing, work benefits, and involvement in the local church both as lay and clergy leaders. Unmarried partners have become increasingly vocal about their rights to tax and medical benefits. These political movements have both influenced the church and been influenced by the church. Liberal and conservative church leaders have weighed in on sexual issues in the arenas of politics, science, and medicine. The results of these justice movements remain to be seen. What voices of morality and ethics will influence sexual values or behaviors in the years ahead?

The moral voice of the church is perceived by the media as too antiquated to be taken seriously. Mainline Christianity, in fact, is greatly threatened by its battles over sexuality. Clergy dubbed the 2000 General Conference of the United Methodist Church in Cleveland, Ohio, "The War on the Shore." The massive attention given to the "war" over sexuality itself provides evidence of the deep layers of personal pain underneath the surface of the combatants. When sexual shame arises in individuals and congregations, the placing of shame on others diverts it. The projection of sexual sin onto groups of people or categories of behavior deepens the damage of shame.

Questions for Reflection

1. William Countryman notes that Christians feel "anxiety about the erotic." What do you think of this statement?
2. What sins go overlooked by the clergy and/or laity of your congregation?
3. What sins are considered the worst?

4. Are sexual sins dealt with differently than the sins of greed or violence?
5. How does the author think that Augustine's personal sexual experience informed his beliefs?
6. Define *sexual justice*.
7. Do you agree with the idea that congregations need to work for sexual justice?
8. Is sexual justice the same as or different from other struggles for justice (for example, racial justice or environmental justice)?

5. Sexual Sin

At a family picnic, when Nancy was five years old, her uncle began putting his hands in unwelcome places. Her younger brother, who was nearby, didn't get help; he simply sat and watched. Nancy was old enough to know that what her uncle was doing to her was wrong but decided in her young mind that it must have been her fault. When she was nine, her fourteen-year-old brother raped her, robbing her not only of virginity but also of love. If people who love you treat you like that, you decide to stop loving people.

I wish I could say this is an unusual story, but it is not. Sometimes the molester is Uncle Harry, Dad, Mom, or a boyfriend on a date. In any event, I can tell you that people like Nancy can and do recover. By taking small steps, they relearn that love and trust are different from abuse and rape. But for many people years of love and abuse are tragically mixed together. There are, in fact, many victims of the mistaken idea that men possess women, children, and their sexuality. When a human being usurps the rights and the power of women or children and justifies it as "my privilege," that is sinful sexual contact.

Whenever genital contact involves an imbalance of power, it is sinful. No adult can have genital or other sexual contact with a child without causing extreme damage. The Christian church has contributed to the disease of incest by teaching that children are possessions and the father is the lord and master of the house. When the parent-child relationship becomes so imbalanced that the parent becomes sexually intimate with the child, we must identify the wrong and grieve for the perpetrators and victims alike. We must also ask if our congregation is the kind of place where a victim could come and talk with a church leader or pastor about family abuse or incest. If not, we have more work to do in order to talk openly about sexual shame.

Confusing Sexual Violence and Intimacy

For too long we have confused sexual violence and sexual intimacy. Violence is power over another, aggression, hostility, and intimidation. Sexual intimacy is shared power, playfulness, love, and risk taking. Sexual violence involves one person co-opting another for sexual pleasure. Sexual intimacy involves mutually agreed upon boundaries and activities.

The church has participated in perpetuating sexual abuse by theologically articulating patriarchy. We have told people that God is the ruler over man and that man is to rule over the woman and children. We have illumined Bible verses where women and children are counted last or not at all and considered property to be used and disposed of as the man sees fit. Our participation, theologically, in family violence contributes to the shame of victims and perpetrators alike.

Aggression and sex: these two drives have been described as the source of all human disorders. Freud claimed that aggression is the foundation of all relations of affection. In Western culture there exists a strong aggressive component in sex and, for some people, a sexual component in aggression. Yet the motivation of such an aggressive and violent act as rape is not sexual pleasure but the desire to degrade and humiliate another and to demonstrate control or domination. Rape is therefore an issue of violence, not sexual intimacy, although the two frequently get mixed together in fantasy and reality.

Pornography and Sexuality

The link between aggression and sexuality is made hazier in our Western patriarchal society by the presence and proliferation of pornography. In this arena conservatives and some feminists are united regarding its damaging influence. The presence of violence in pornography is so widespread that the government is now able to prosecute those who produce or sell the most graphically violent sexual films. Some research has suggested that films linking sexual arousal and the infliction of pain increase the number and severity of cases of actual violence against women and children. Moreover, we are facing an explosion of sexually explicit materials on the Internet. I am not suggesting that we repress healthy erotic literature; I am saying that if we use pornographic material to separate sexuality from interpersonal intimacy, we create a dangerous split between persons and their own bodies.

We hear a lot about how pornography degrades women, but it also degrades men. While pornography promotes male fantasies of power over the powerless, it also promotes self-destructive attitudes in men. By providing substitute gratification, it provides an escape for individuals seeking to avoid relating to their partners in fully human and respectful ways. Pornography also encourages unrealistic sexual expectations for both men and women. Women are expected to look and act like Playboy bunnies, and men are expected to be super studs with large sexual organs that can be instantly aroused. Shame, then, appears in the space between the ideal of what we should or want to be and our experience of ourselves. Pornography and shame result from the dichotomy of media-hyped sexual images and our true selves.

As I noted previously, sometimes people who feel low and unworthy actually repeat a behavior over and over again in an effort to rid themselves of the shame. A single mother goes to a Christian therapist because she is sexually active, though not ready for a long-term committed relationship. She believes that her active sexual life is wrong and an abomination in the sight of God. She wants to know why she is going against her own beliefs. This feeling of shame doesn't stop her; in fact, it compels her into the act. She has an unconscious thought that if she tries it again and again, she will stop feeling shame about it. This cycle is often at the core of repeat offenders of various kinds of sexual abuse.

Another abuse resulting from pornography is detachment. No loneliness is greater than a sexual encounter without intimacy. Donald Goergen writes:

> Sexual arousal is not the same as love and the two need to be clearly distinguished. Sexual arousal, attractions, and desires do not imply love for another person by whom we are aroused or to whom we are attracted. Too often we confuse the two.[1]

As we seek to be fulfilled persons, we seek relationship as well as sexual release. Only one or the other, and we come up empty.

Biblical Pornography

I have defined *sexual sin* as that which destroys self-worth, the use of one's body for power over another, seeing ourselves or others as only objects of pleasure, and engaging in physical acts that increase our shame or another's shame before God. If we accept this definition of sexual sin and that our culture confuses violence with intimacy, we can see that the Bible has been used in just as damaging a way as magazines purchased in adult bookstores. How can this be?

The church has used the "laws" of some biblical texts to shame people. Other biblical "laws" have been long ago rejected. For example, no preacher today steps into the pulpit and goes on at length about couples having sex while the female partners are menstruating. No one talks of "the sin of masturbation" any longer.

Linking sexual activity with original sin, however, is the epitome of shaming theology. As will be discussed in the next chapter, original sin and the fall are not biblically linked. This confusion has led to centuries of tight constrictions regarding human sexual behavior.

The Catholic church has maintained the virginal holiness ideal in its teachings about Mary, Mother of God. The church also reinforces shame by its defense of celibacy in the priesthood and among nuns. Protestants are strongly influenced by these voices of Christian teaching. The shaming of those who choose to be sexually expressive outside of the civil laws of marriage, for example, continues in all branches of Christianity. George Bernard Shaw once slyly remarked, "Why should we take advice on sex from the Pope? If he knows anything about it, he shouldn't."[2] More recently, Matt Groening, in his comic strip "Life in Hell," wrote, "When authorities warn you of the sinfulness of sex, there is an important lesson to be learned. Do not have sex with the authorities."[3]

The Protestant reformers didn't exactly clear the way for shame-free sexual expression. Luther and Calvin both made lists of sexual sins in the order of their severity. Luther called sexual intercourse between husband and wife a "venial sin," a sin "God winks at." Unfortunately, while God may have been winking at this "sin," the very naming of it as such helped fuel the sexual revolution of the past few decades. And the backlash against this degradation of a human drive continues. While Christianity has presumed authority on all aspects of life, including sexuality, for nearly two thousand years, psychology, a relative newcomer on the stage of history, argues that sexuality is an unconscious drive and an ordinary hunger. This, of course, doesn't easily erase or change two thousand years of teaching, during which the church has frequently been confused, ambiguous, and silent on the subject of human sexuality.

Alongside thousands of years of theological sexual norms, then, are one hundred years of scientific research leading to current understandings of sexual behavior. Biblical condemnations of same-gendered sex (as misinterpreted as they often are) underlie most Protestant teachings even today. At the same time, scientists have revealed that sexual orientation is not the fixed and rigid line we once believed it was. Healthy individuals relate with affection to members of both their own sex and the opposite. Sexuality is not prescribed by cultural expectations of what is masculine or what is feminine, nor do these expectations restrict it. On the forefront of sexual genetics are studies suggesting that sexual orientation is biologically determined and randomly inherited.[4]

The deep shame felt by and about homosexual and bisexual people is described in several places in this text. For an in-depth look at homosexual shame, I would recommend reading Gershen Kaufman and Lev Raphael's *Coming Out of Shame: Transforming Gay and Lesbian Lives.*[5] We need to be clear that labeling an orientation or entire categories of sexual behavior as sinful serves no good purpose. It does not reinforce monogamy or affirm the sacramental nature of human love but simply shames the individuals who engage in it. Moreover, the church has decried homosexuals and bisexuals for their supposed promiscuity while ignoring the promiscuity of their own leaders. No wonder, then, that people have fled the church in search of integrity and affirmation.

One Congregation's Perpetuation of Shame

Many pastors and churches have refused same-sex couples the rite of marriage or holy union. Such couples are, consequently, excluded from rituals that would pronounce them faithful in the eyes of God and, instead, shamed for their "promiscuity." Before one couple came to a new congregation that agreed to marry them, they had belonged to two other congregations that refused to do so. The previous congregations "let us serve coffee at the fellowship hour and help with the youth group, but they didn't let us marry." The couple explained, "We want to be married because we are uncomfortable with the way that some members of the lesbian community don't take fidelity seriously. We want to be witnesses to the kind of love that Jesus shows us in the Bible."

I learned that this couple was also parenting a thirteen-year-old daughter. Refusal to marry them would have resulted in the daughter being shamed as well. It would have been like saying, "Your mothers are sinners; they are unworthy to be married in the sight of God." We don't say that to children whose parents may have had sexual intercourse outside of marriage or to children whose parents ended a previous marriage because of adultery. Yet the children of gay and lesbian parents receive the shame that the church places on their parents.

Virginia Ramey Mollenkott explains that carnal ways of relating include treating one another as possessions or privileges, perpetrating acts of violence, engaging in sexuality in a detached and lonely way, and relating to one another out of fear and judgment.[6] If I may paraphrase the apostle Paul in a letter to the Corinthian congregation:

> You know your bodies are parts of the body of Christ. Shall I take a part of Christ's body and use it unfeelingly? Shall I reduce the fullness of life to an encounter without meaning, in which I relieve my sexual tension only to find I am lonely for human love? Become instead spiritually one with the Lord. Avoid immorality. Don't sin against your own body. Don't you know that your body is a temple of the Holy Spirit within you, which you have from God, and that you are not your own? (1 Cor. 6:19)

The church's task is to call people into relationships within the context of love. We don't need shame to do this. We do, however, need to articulate the goals of fidelity and sanctification and to honor the sacramental nature of sexuality. We need to affirm human relationships in which sexual intimacy uplifts, upholds, and creates communion.

David Mace writes that the process of healing from sexual shame "will involve us in the honest examination of sexual relationships we have prejudged without examination. I do not say that we must now condone what we have in the past condemned. What I do say is that we must abandon the habit of prejudging without examination."[7]

Affirming Sexuality in the Christian Context

Leo Buscaglia, popular author and speaker, received six hundred responses to a questionnaire he sent to people with successful and long-lasting relationships. He asked that they list the qualities of a good relationship. Do you think sex was number one, two, or in the top five? The category "romance and sex" actually came in at number eight, behind communication, affection, forgiveness, honesty, vulnerability, dependability, and a sense of humor.[8] Are you surprised?

If we look at Christian sexuality in a shame-free context, we will begin with conversation about what makes sex good and what makes good sex. Good sex is communication, affection, forgiveness, honesty, vulnerability, dependability, and a sense of humor. How good would sex be without these qualities? While good sex can be tender, healing, and somber, it is also sometimes raucous and playful. The animal kingdom reminds us of the joy of sex. Consider the proud peacock or the turkey, about whom Ogden Nash writes (with parallels to human experience): "There's nothing more perky than a masculine turkey. When he struts he struts with no ifs or buts. When his face is apoplectic his harem grows hectic, and when he gobbles their universe wobbles."[9] We can but wonder and rejoice and beware of the attractions we have for one another. And while it may be simple for the animals—the birds and the bees—it is very complex for human beings.

Sexuality involves the complexity of our emotional lives; yet when society talks of sex, it usually talks narrowly of genital stimulation and release. The latter is only one component of our sexual intimacy but is given the most attention. While good genital sex is highly erotic, warm, intimate, playful, and pleasurable, it is only in a context of love and commitment that it also produces a sense of being one with self, the other, and with God.

Our sexual intimacy involves the quality of love and openness we have with one another. It includes a goal shared, a good belly laugh, a tender touch or caress at the end of the day. And when or if we add good genital sex to sexual intimacy, the Lord is praised all the more. I heard of a husband who always had prayer with his wife before having sex, and I was curious to know about that. It turns out that his prayer is the table grace I grew up with: "O Lord, for what we are about to receive, may we be truly thankful."

If you have someone in your life who will greet you with open arms, you have intimacy. Unfortunately, we tend to define the world by what we don't have rather than what we do have. Single persons maintain healthy sexual lives through self-love, celibacy, and/or carefully choosing safe and monogamous sexual partners. Many a couple has a deeply sexual relationship into their older years. And even when genital dysfunction is a problem, there are other ways to be sexually intimate.

The problem with our cultural treatment of sex is that we have come to think that sex is always orgasmic. Sometimes it is, and sometimes it isn't. We should no more expect every encounter in bed to bring on stars and whistles and bells than we expect every meal we cook to be a big hit with the family. Sometimes sex is great, sometimes just average, and sometimes poor. But you don't quit the team when you lose a game or two, right? You keep on practicing, you strategize together, you get in shape for it, you get a coach if you have to. But you stay loyal to the team. I'm talking now about the crucial importance of commitment.

One Sunday after I had preached a sermon about sexuality, an older man in the church took me aside in the narthex. He told me that every time he was in a dangerous situation about his sexuality, the power of Jesus Christ worked in him and kept him from "sin." He was attracted to another woman and could not by his own power keep from pursuing a relationship with her. Once, in a real moment of temptation in a hotel room with her, he actually prayed for release and then confessed to her that he could not continue, having been freed from his own desires. I had never heard a clearer story about the power of prayer to protect against sexual shame.

For adults as well as teens, a "Just Say No" campaign is too simplistic to protect individuals from dangerous situations. While there have always been high emotional risks, risk of pregnancy, and the loss of social esteem at stake for those who want to be sexually active, the additional risk of AIDS has resulted in the tragic loss of too many young lives. Being responsible about one's sexuality involves self-awareness, the freedom to say no, and the obligations that go along with saying yes.

Developing Your Own Sexual Ethic

In a time when boundaries have blurred regarding sin and sex, each person is left to make his or her own decisions about sexual behavior. Denominations and congregations need to involve themselves in the discussion of sexual ethics and provide guidelines for ethical living and loving. For example, the United Church of Christ published a thorough study on human sexuality,[10] which includes a list of the elements involved in making a moral decision. Questions that could be considered before a sexual encounter are:

- Am I motivated by love for this person and myself?
- Will this act produce human fulfillment and wholeness?
- Will this act contribute to my relationship with God?
- What will be the consequence of this act?
- Am I committed to the depth of intimacy with this person that a sexual encounter will produce?
- Have I done everything possible to protect myself and my lover from the risk of sexually transmitted diseases?
- Will I be fully responsible if a pregnancy happens?
- Will I be able to tell others whom I love about this intimate relationship?

By looking clearly at the intention and the consequences of sexual encounters, we develop standards about our sexual acts based in love, as we understand it through Jesus Christ. We can teach our children about sexuality and biblical moral standards by emphasizing love, commitment, and consequence. We don't need to shame them in order to teach them. We can teach them to value good communication in sex by the way we ourselves communicate with them about sex.

Many of us received little or no guidance from our parents about sex. In the movie *Peggy Sue Got Married* the mother gives her a short speech on the night of the prom: "You know what a penis is, Peggy Sue—stay away from it."[11] But there is more to it than that. Parents and educators must start early in discussing sexuality with their children. They would do well to learn what their schools are teaching children about sex and to find out if any kind of ethics component is included. Parents also need to support schools in teaching safer sex and in affirming the dignity of all persons.

A divorced and separated group in our community included education about condom use in its curriculum. Did the group include discussions about sexual ethics, what is sin and what isn't? No. These topics still scare people in churches. Yet post-divorce singles are in great need of defining their sexual intimacy in new ways. Terms like *celibacy, serial monogamy,* and *guidelines for dating and sex* are new to divorced people in their midlife years. Again, if groups in churches provided Christians with ways to discuss their own ethical considerations without shame, spirituality and sexuality would remain intact.

Christian parents may need to risk embarrassing themselves a little by talking to their kids about sex. They need to answer questions about sex at every stage of development. And as soon as young people feel sexual attraction during puberty, parents can tell them, "Yes, sex is wonderful. It's like a sacrament that God gives us for each other." Parents can tell them how powerfully wonderful, and yet how dangerous, it is. They can tell them that saying no is still okay and that saying yes means keeping sex safe and responsible.

Education for preteens about sexuality also needs to include an alcohol and drug education component. Recent studies have shown that teens as early as age twelve are having casual, unprotected sex when drinking. The availability of alcohol is key. On the other hand, studies also show that those who abstain from alcohol and sex have been counseled by their parents not to engage in those activities.

I urge parents to tell their children that the church has often been wrong about sex in the past and even more often has been silent on the issue. I urge parents to study the Scriptures with their teens, discussing both the context and the content of the writing. I urge them to talk frequently about Jesus' law of love and his ability to love and challenge saints, sinners, and ordinary buffoons like us.

Youths need us to teach them how to use their bodies as temples of God and signs of God's love. We can begin with our children to bring sex and religion back together. Sexual intimacy is bound up with our need for love and understanding, consideration and compassion, loyalty and constancy, integrity, trust, and holiness. God gives us the opportunity and the responsibility to love. We don't need to use shame to teach about sex or to enforce rules against it.

Questions for Reflection

1. How would you define *sexual sin?* Can your study group agree on a single definition?
2. What does the media's portrayal of sexual violence communicate?
3. Does pornography contribute to sexual shame? How?
4. Is monogamy a thing of the past?
5. Look again at the United Church of Christ publication's list of elements involved in making a moral decision. How might you use this list?

6. Revisiting the Garden

A closer look at the mixed messages the church conveys about sexuality might prove helpful. The principle story cited by nearly every book on sexuality and theology is the creation story. Man and woman are created in God's likeness. God honors them as sexual beings, and they are looked on as being good. Genesis 2:25 says, "And the man and his wife were both naked, and were not ashamed."

It Wasn't about Sex

A mixed message in Genesis grows out of the story of the fall. At first Adam and Eve were naked and unashamed. Then, after the fall, they covered themselves and hid in the garden, deeply ashamed. The shame of Adam and Even in the garden has long been incorrectly interpreted to be shame related to their sexuality. But God did not catch them having sex. Instead, they disobeyed God's command not to eat of the tree of the knowledge of good and evil. They ate of this tree, thinking it would make them equal with God. This is the source of their downfall. Interest in each other's bodies isn't evident here; their lust to be like God is the source of their idealism and their shame.

In a review of Christian theology and shame, John Berecz and Herbert Helm Jr. describe the danger of wanting to become equal with God.[1] As Adam and Eve strove to become like God themselves, they faced the shame of falling far short of the goal. "You will not surely die," the serpent said to the woman, "for God knows that when you eat of it your eyes will be opened, and you will be like God, knowing good and evil" (Gen. 3:4-8). Berecz and Helm conclude: "It is in attempting to be 'like God' that we generate the highest levels of shame. The first recorded instances of shame occurred immediately following humankind's attempt to move into the realm of Godliness."

Seen from a psychological perspective, Adam and Eve failed both to live up to God's expectations for them and their own expectations of themselves; thus the beginning of shame. Yet for centuries the church has infused this story with bizarre sexual connotations. Art and advertising depict what happened in the Garden in ways that reinforce gender stereotypes, denigrate women, and foster sales of products. The Garden is seen as the ultimate metaphor for seduction. The woman gets mixed up with the evil snake, and the man emerges as a character entirely out of control in the presence of the temptress. No one in the Garden takes responsibility for his or her own behavior, and blaming protects them both from the shame they feel in the aftermath.

The Genesis story is the source of the debate about sex and procreation. Some Christians place bumper stickers on their cars that read, "It was Adam and Eve, not Adam and Steve." Those who see heterosexuality as the only acceptable sexuality in the sight of God often base this on the Genesis text. The Hebrew belief that the male line must be preserved at all costs led to a consistent Old Testament teaching that sexual intercourse was only to be affirmed if it produced children. This meant that men were expected to use concubines, to sleep with their dead brother's wives, to go to temple prostitutes, and even to use their own daughters in order to preserve the blood line. Women, as the holding vessel for male seed, were required to keep their wombs available only to their husbands, and they were divorced if children could not be produced.

Hebrew Love Poetry

To understand sexuality in the biblical context, one needs to read the incredible poetry of the Song of Songs (sometimes referred to as the Song of Solomon). Here the poet links soul-filled loving with all of the senses and all of one's being. "Your lips are like crimson thread, and your mouth is lovely. Your cheeks are like halves of a pomegranate behind your veil. . . . Your breasts are like two fawns, twins of a gazelle that feed among the lilies" (Song of Songs 4:3, 5). This book is a celebration of God's creation of love and sexuality. The love described here springs out of our human nature but is very much connected to the heart of God. Sensual love as well as the love of God contains mystery, wonder, and deep joy.

A unique aspect of the Song is that more than half of its verses are ascribed to a female voice. This is the only book in the Bible in which the female voice predominates.

> In fact, the protagonist's voice in Song of Songs is the only unmediated female voice in all of Scripture. . . . The book's pro-

nounced and unrelenting female point of view is reinforced further by its strong female imagery. The presence of such important female imagery allows Song of Songs to be seen as a collection of meditations from a woman's heart.[2]

For generations the church has been ashamed to acknowledge that the Song is overtly sexual. Its lack of direct reference to God has made it suspect, and some commentators have tried to discredit its placement in the biblical canon or have tried to ignore it altogether. How many church Bible study groups are familiar with this text?

Scholars throughout the centuries have reduced the Song of Songs to mundane reflections on humanity and God. Evelyn and James Whitehead write:

> The Song of Songs celebrates the realm of sexual pleasure as a gift of creation. But to many Jews and Christians this was going too far. . . . Scandalized by this book, they searched for an interpretation that could avoid its obvious erotic content. Their search led to allegory. Nearly all Jewish and Christian interpreters have viewed this poem as an allegory, describing either God's love for the human soul or Christ's love for the Church. Its message, they argue, is about spiritual affection, not about human erotic love![3]

Commentators have gone to great lengths to interpret the references to breasts as allegorical illustrations about the mountains and the image of the arrival of the young stag as an allegory for the arrival of spring.

The overt references to the body throughout the text have been downplayed.

> With abandon, the lovers in Song of Songs delight in the physical pleasures of love. They revel in each other's body: taste (2:3; 4:11; 5:1), touch (7:6-9), smell (1:12-14; 4:16), and the sound (2:8, 14; 5:16) of each other's voice. The female body poses no ethical problems in Song of Songs, although in other parts of Scripture it is problematic. It bleeds (cf. Leviticus 12; 15:19-30); it breeds (Leviticus 12); it confounds male wisdom (Numbers 5); and it has enormous power over the male imagination (Lev. 21:7; cf. 2 Samuel 11), or so it seems.[4]

Sexual shame evidences itself in earlier interpretations of this and other stories in biblical literature. Attempts to desexualize the content of the text of the Song of Songs are akin to the "no talk" rules of families with sexual secrets. Luckily more recent research has opened the text again to shine forth as a full and sensual poem on the nature of sexual love.[5]

The power of the Song of Songs and its controversies became clear to me when I decided to preach on it for Valentine's Day in 1996. In a sermon titled "The Erotic Love of God," I outlined the sensual pleasure described in the Song's poetry. I noted that most Sunday school teachers do not mention this book's presence in the Bible. I noted for the congregation that this book could be considered the "centerfold" of the Scriptures. Luckily, they laughed.

About a week after the sermon, the critiques started pouring into the office. We shouldn't talk about sex in church. Valentine's Day isn't a Christian holiday. What would our teenagers think about the fact that the preacher was talking about sex in the pulpit? The teens were thrilled, of course. But a group of older women became quite disturbed by the sermon and its content.

As is the custom in our congregation, the sermon had been recorded on videotape for our members who are "shut-ins." One of the older matriarchs checked out the video from the church office and invited a group of her friends to watch it at her home. Some of them had been away that Sunday, and she felt it was her obligation to fill them in on what had happened in church. The women gathered, and she ranted about the preacher. But the event backfired on her. In fact, I received several calls later that week from people telling me "it was about time" someone admitted that people have pleasurable feelings about sex and that even the Bible thinks it's okay.

The funny postscript of the story is that the tape vanished. Rumor had it that some people were still circulating it around town, showing it to friends and fellow complainers. The office staff joked that I had now produced the first X-rated video the church had ever had. That sermon's half-life was longer than any of my other sermons. Why? Because it broke the taboos of shame and addressed sexuality from a perspective of healthy and value-centered love.

More Scriptural References

As preachers attempt to rid themselves and the church of sexual shame, the opening of Scripture to new interpretations is vital. There are lists of sexual sins in Scripture, some of which are now common practices by most Christians, and others of which are singled out as the most shameful of the list. We don't tell adulterers that they won't be ordained in the church or can't hold office. We don't ask new members if they have intercourse during their menstrual cycles. Yet we have developed a post-textual hierarchy of sins based on the ones that hold the greatest shame attachment throughout the prevailing secular and Christian culture.

We wish that Jesus had said more about sexuality, but he says nothing directly about it. The most often-cited references for Jesus' opinion about sexual sin are the stories about the Samaritan woman and the woman caught in adultery. These stories lack the fuller picture of the involvement of the men in these women's lives. The Samaritan woman had been found in the "very act" (John 8:4) of adultery, but the man in that "very act" never appears in the scene. He is freed of shame by the cultural privilege of being male. To the woman about to be stoned, Jesus says, "Let anyone among you who is without sin be the first to throw a stone at her" (John 8:7). Jesus offers an unequivocal ethic against blame. Her shame is relieved, and her life is restored.

The Samaritan woman is asked to return to her community and stop sinning. In a culture where multiple partnerships were accepted, one isn't clear from the story exactly what sins the woman is expected to clean up. Some accounts say that afterward the Samaritan woman went home and became an influential witness for Jesus. Jesus confronted other characters about their sins, including the rich man to whom he said, "Go, sell your possessions, and give the money to the poor" (Matt. 19:21). Why is it that Christians have focused on the sins of the "flesh," even reading some of them into the texts, but have left the other directives go? Jesus made it clear that all of the laws of the Hebrew Scriptures had to be measured against the law of love. He advocated equality and social and class justice. He was unafraid of those whom others considered "tainted" by sexual condemnation or by diseases of the body or spirit.

Jesus avoided self-loathing of any kind and avoided shaming in all of his personal encounters. His direct style and loving confrontations opened a path to healing. When the woman with the alabaster jar anointed his feet and dried them with her hair, his disciples were horrified. Jesus was respectful. In another instance, not only did he speak to the man in the tree (Zachaeus), but he asked if he could join him for dinner (Luke 19:2-5).

Over and over again we find Jesus willing to be among those whom others had condemned. The crippled and blind, the tax collector, and the leper were all welcomed into his healing. His respectful treatment of all people (even the demons and the hypocrites) stands as a model for our behavior today. In his teaching, prophetic witness, and chastisement, he stays focused on the actions—what you think in your heart can be as dangerous as what you do with your body—and away from character.

The apostle Paul's writings tended to confuse the church on issues of sexuality and spirituality. For example, Paul considered that love of Christ must always preempt sexual love and that the two were opposed to one anther. Thanks to Paul and the early church fathers, a dualism arose that claimed that love of God and human sexual love were incompatible. They taught that holiness required reining in one's sexual desires, thereby pitting a life of faith against a life of active sexual expression. Dualism focused on the fall as the source of sexual lust and cited the virgin birth as proof that women chosen by God are to be pure, chaste virgins. Dualism also used the celibacy of Paul and Jesus as proof that the renunciation of sex is the only way of life that pleases God and that those who engage in sex sink to an inferior spiritual level. Paul's contribution to the issue of sexual shame cannot be denied. His writings reinforced slavery and racial injustice and limited women's voices in the church for thousands of years. His words now reinforce the dominant culture's bent toward shame. Only when Paul is seen as a man struggling with his own sexuality in light of his commitment to serving the church do we manage to set his comments in context and understand them fully.

Questions for Reflection

1. Do you think that trying to be like God is a sin?
2. Do people who try to be like Christ end up feeling shame? If so, why?
3. Do you feel ashamed of feelings of anger, fear, doubt, or pride? Do you think those feelings are unchristian?
4. How has "procreation-only" sexuality influenced your faith community?
5. What do you think needs to be said or not to be said from the pulpit about sexuality?
6. The author says that "Jesus avoided self-loathing of any kind and avoided shaming in all of his personal encounters." Do you agree or disagree? Why?

7. Gender and Shame

The theological underpinnings of women's shame reaches back to the concept of virginity as the purest and holiest state for women before God. Women who were virgins were both honored and feared. Men both longed for women whose purity was still intact and hated them because they were so highly dangerous. Throughout the history of Christianity, women have been given the option of being spiritual and not sexual or sexual but not spiritual. Around 200 C.E. Tertullian wrote of woman: "You are the devil's gateway; you are the unsealer of that forbidden tree; you are the first deserter of the Divine Law. . . . You destroyed so easily God's image, man. On account of your desertions—that is death—even the Son of God had to die."[1]

Freud and Gender

Much of Sigmund Freud's early work was with women who had been abused as children. Unfortunately, Freud planted the seeds of sexual shame by focusing on the victim's symptoms rather than on the system that fostered the abuse. Freud studied the women's lives with particular attention to manifestations of their stress, coining the term *hysteria*, which, like *hysterectomy*, is related to the female body. The later-used term *hysterical conversion* describes intense emotional expression. While women's symptoms today might be considered traumatic responses to early sexual shame, in Freud's day women were singled out and doubly shamed.[2]

Some of Freud's peers and later students of psychology drew sweeping conclusions that women have a great deal more shame than men.[3] This coincides with the perception that women have borne the sexual shame of the culture. They have been labeled temptresses, whores, and sluts. Women's bodies have been treated as properties of others. Women's "no" has been trivialized. Women's physical health in childbirth has been overridden by men's need for sexual satisfaction and their desire to perpetuate the lineage. Women have been labeled with titles that degrade them and then blamed for having more shame than the other gender. The treatment of women's shame for the past century has been slow to take into account the interwoven dynamics among gender, power, and abuse.

Geoffrey May explains: "In attempting to desexualize the idea of man, ascetic (early) Christianity succeeded only in oversexualizing the idea of woman." The oversexualizing of women is clear in media and marketing campaigns, news reporting, politics, and yes, faith communities. How does the oversexualizing of women affect you and your congregation?

Clergy and Gender

Issues of gender and shame appear throughout the life of the church. Pastoral leaders experience such issues acutely. In the early 1990s the Bishop of the United Methodist California/Nevada Conference held a series of required meetings to educate clergy about issues of sexual conduct. At these gatherings clergy freely expressed their confusion about their own sexual boundaries in the church. Many of the men talked about having to be neutered in the expression of their masculinity. Because the role of clergy is a softer, more "feminine" role, many of the men felt that this restricted their instinctive and culturally trained machismo. Male humor, for example, so prevalent in the locker room and on prime-time sitcoms, is unacceptable in the pulpit.

One of the participants told the story about having his ear pierced. His congregation was aghast. For them, the earring symbolized a cross-gender identification they weren't prepared to deal with. They feared that he might be gay. Their ultimate concern that he might cross gender barriers was too deep to express. And consequently they shamed him.

The clergy agreed that the church very subtly restricts their humor, their physical movement and touch, and their words regarding sex. A man nearing his retirement concluded, "I think that clergy wear robes so that they become genderless." His experience rang true for all of the workshop participants. Clergy struggle with sexual repression and shame. As leaders, the ways that clergy deal with sexuality have profound effects on individuals and congregations.

The presence of the female gender in church leadership has put a whole new slant on the tension between women as sex objects and women as moral mothers. I was the twenty-fifth woman ordained and sent out to preach in my conference in the late 1970s. When female leadership stepped into the pulpit, sexuality-related topics were broached sometimes for the first time. Since women have been oversexualized, they have a harder time appearing neutered and genderless as the male clergy before them did. Women, by virtue of pregnancy and childbirth, are obvious about their sexual activity! Congregations couldn't ignore the sexuality of their young pastors who were also nursing mothers. Women becoming Christlike leaders in the 1970s and 80s challenged the church's repression of sexuality. The old options for women of being either virgins or whores are at odds with clergywomen as leaders and preachers. Into which category does the new preacher fall? This oversimplified statement is intended to highlight the complexity of the deeper issues. Congregations have found themselves facing gender and sexuality issues in the last few decades, alongside the statistical rise in the numbers of clergywomen in church leadership. The fault line is shifting in relation to the gender shift of pastoral leaders in the church.

The shame of women leaders is worked out differently than the shame of male leaders. Gender shame is experienced differently in the culture and in the home. Women's shame may be evident in chronic depression, anxiety, and eating disorders. Among clergy, women's sexual shame may manifest itself in a lack of self-esteem and in tentative leadership. Men's shame is unspoken and often (especially in the church) deeply repressed, emerging as addiction or compulsive sexual fantasy or activity. The church has attracted highly charismatic and self-absorbed male leaders. These narcissistic characteristics can lead to sexual misconduct. Both of these responses to shame affect the sexual and spiritual well-being of the faith community.

A look at men and shame reveals that men are particularly shamed for certain feelings. It's acceptable to be angry but not to be sad. It's okay to feel contempt but not fear. And for men, the prohibitions against touching leave them without the physical healing potential of touch without sexual arousal. Our culture has limited men's touching to the bedroom. We have assumed that men's touch is always sexual, thus shaming them for their basic need for human holding and stroking. As Gershen Kaufman notes, "The only times it's okay for men to touch are on the gridiron, in the midst of contest, or at the bar after a few drinks. Then anyone can touch, and it doesn't count, because we're not responsible. Or maybe at the airport, where you can hug or touch anybody, so long as it's brief."[4] The shame men feel regarding their needs for intimacy, softness, and relatedness is experienced daily.

Some clergymen experience shame about their professions in light of spirituality having been given to the "feminine" and the caregiving roles in culture having been filled primarily by women. There are ample doses of gender shame that affect both men and women.

Expanding Gender Constructs

Thus far, this discussion of gender and shame has been based on the two primary genders in our culture. It should be noted that there are persons who are morphologically both male and female and persons who have a physical body that is one gender and a mental and emotional self that is the opposite.[5] Most churches are ill prepared to deal with the blurring of gender lines. At All Souls Community Church in San Francisco, however, leaders realized that they could not be welcoming of all people while the restrooms still restricted gender to "men" and "women." They took down the gender signs and put locks on individual stalls.

When a transgendered woman became a music leader at another congregation, a couple who were active in the church dropped out. They said that her skirt was too short; they felt extreme discomfort about the mix-up of genders they saw in front of them. The congregation bid them a warm good-bye and continued to invite the music leader to play the guitar on Sunday. When she speaks to groups of people now about the transformation from male to female that took place over a two-year period, she says that she was blessed and surprised to find that Christ ministered to her through that church.

Our culture is only beginning to study and understand gender. In many other cultures religious leaders are considered gender-free. Shaman and Native American healers are often said to embody both sexes. *Androgyny* is a word that our culture is beginning to accept; it means that persons can have the best of both gender identifications within them, no matter their physical anatomy. Your congregation or study group might gain further understanding of gender issues through viewing and discussing a recent Belgian film, *Ma Vie en Rose*.[6] The film is about a young boy who believes himself to be a girl who was mistakenly given a boy's body. The responses of his parents and the community accurately tell the sad and touching story of many transgendered individuals. If you view the film, notice the place where shame is the primary feeling.

Our freedom and respect for one another call us to open our minds to gender issues alongside sexual issues. When we feel queasy about someone's looks or behavior, when we feel disgust, or when we think "that's not normal," we have entered the portal of shame. It may be our own shame or it may be cultural shame, but these feelings indicate that more reflection is needed. If we can stop ourselves at that moment and ask more questions, live with the tension, or humbly ask for insight from God, we will reduce our tendency to shame.

Shmuley Boteach, recent winner of the *London Times* preaching contest, wrote this message to us about religion and shame: "The only true test of my love of G-d is the degree to which I love his children. The ancient Jewish mystics taught that G-d is in hiding in our world. The only way to find Him is to connect with his image in this world, our human brothers and sisters."[7] When the limitations of our own gender, the strange mysteries of another gender, or the complexity of multi-gendered people challenges us, we have the opportunity to bring God out of hiding too.

Questions for Reflection

1. Discuss Geoffrey May's comment that we have "oversexualized" women.
2. Do you think your congregation has a dress code? If so, what is it?
3. Why do you think the pastor's earring bothered his parishioners?
4. The author suggests that sexual issues are being raised in congregations more often now that women have become pastors. Do you agree or disagree, and why?
5. All Souls Community Church decided that the signs for "men" and "women" on the bathrooms were limiting. Discuss this in your group.
6. How would your congregation react to having a transgendered guitarist leading worship music?
7. How do you know what gender you are?
8. Discuss with your group the possibility that God is gender-free.
9. Where might God be "in hiding" in your congregation?

8. When the Pastor Is Ashamed

In literature and film, stories of sexual infidelity by clergy romanticize the breaking of taboos. Recall the popularity of *The Thorn Birds*, a made-for-television film about the affair of a Catholic priest. The fact that a recent film was based on Nathaniel Hawthorne's classic text about shame, *The Scarlet Letter*, suggests that the breaking of the taboos remains a popular theme. The more strict the taboo, the more alluring the indiscretion.

The role of pastor has within it the expectation of purity. While the laity are expected to be Christlike, they receive less shame for not achieving that goal than clergy do. As spokespersons for God, religious leaders are laden with the burden of shame if they do not embody the congregation's strictest moral codes. Throughout the centuries ordination requirements have included behavioral contracts around drinking, card playing, and gambling. The sexual rules were not overtly covered, since everyone "knew" what was expected of clergy.

Clergy and Narcissism

Most congregations expect their clergy to live a perfect life. By keeping silent on all issues related to sexuality, the congregation coconspires to cover up sexual indiscretion and fosters psychological narcissism. Clergy may be drawn to the parish because of their narcissistic tendencies, or these leanings may be fostered within the dynamics of the congregation. Alexander Lowen writes:

> Narcissism describes both a psychological and a cultural condition. On the individual level, it denotes a personality disturbance characterized by an exaggerated investment in one's image at the expense of the self. . . . On the cultural level, narcissism can be seen in a loss of human values—in a lack of concern . . . for one's fellow human beings.[1]

The narcissist who acts out sexually is full of sexual shame.

Narcissism is based on the Greek myth of Narcissus, a handsome young man who fell in love with Echo, a nymph. Because

Echo was cursed with a lack of speech, Narcissus eventually rejected her, and she died of a broken heart. He was punished by the gods for his callous treatment of Echo; they caused him to fall in love with his own image. Seeing his own reflection in the waters of a fountain, he fell passionately in love with it. He refused to leave the spot and died there, becoming a flower that grows on the edges of springs.

Freud saw narcissism as a healthy stage of sexual development.[2] Yet this is a stage that one needs to grow out of to reach maturity. If the self-aggrandizement of the early years is not balanced by childhood experiences of humility, the condition worsens, rendering the individual incapable of empathy and likely to engage in shameful and shaming behaviors.

Mike's Story

An example may help to illustrate the way that sexual wounds in children can result in adult narcissistic disorders. A fine young man from an East Coast community decided during his high school years to go to seminary. Mike had been raised in the church. Many aspects of pastoral ministry appealed to him. He liked the idea of standing in front of all those people and preaching. He liked the idea of being in charge of a congregation. Mike completed his theological degree, got married, and began a successful career as a parish minister. It was years later that he began, with intensive therapy, to understand that his attraction to pastoral leadership was his attempt to rid himself of the shame he had borne since adolescence.

Mike had grown up in a family of sexual secrets. His father had kept the picture of a girlfriend in his wallet alongside his mother's picture. His mother's attitude about sex was Victorian: It was a necessary evil in order to have children. It wasn't spoken about, and she had deeply repressed her own sexual feelings. She was a product of her time and of the shame of his father's other love.

She raised two fine boys by strict rules about conduct, including swearing. When Mike's older brother said the "f word," she literally washed his mouth out with soap. Mike grew into his early teens having been taught that sex was bad. He had one confiscated copy of a Playboy magazine hidden so cleverly that his mom couldn't possibly find it. He viscerally knew the terror of her reproach should she ever find it. He was also a normal growing boy.

One summer morning Mike was full of pleasure. He was having a healthy, normal, fun morning, learning about how his body and his mind functioned. Mike was masturbating. It was a joy to experience that it all worked, just as his friends had said and just as the movies had suggested. That summer morning, however, Mike's mother didn't knock on his door before entering his room. Mike was exposed. They were both terror-stricken. He covered himself immediately and hung his head for the onslaught. "You dirty rotten boy," she began. "God will punish you for this, you will rot in hell for this." Her voice rose higher and higher. "I am disgusted with you. If I ever find you doing *that* again. . . ." She paused and could not go on. She started to leave the room. "Wait," Mike said, his voice weak and strained, "please don't tell anyone." She glowered at him over her reading glasses. "Please, Mom, I won't do it again, I promise. I know it was bad—just don't tell anyone; promise me." By this time Mike was sobbing out his shame. She was softening. "Alright, Mike, alright."

She closed the door and Mike hugged his knees up under his chin wishing he could die just from the wishing. He wondered if he could ever get the dirty feeling off of his hands or out of his heart again. He stretched out on his bed facedown and thought it over for a long, long time. The scene bore deeper into his soul. That night when Mike's father came home, his mother immediately told him what had happened. This added betrayal to shame. His father never spoke to him about it; he just grounded Mike for a month. The stony silence was another form of shame, and Mike didn't miss that fact.

Mike had engaged in a normal rite of passage for young people. Acute shame and stony silence canceled his curiosity and pleasure. The incident deeply wounded him and set in motion a life pattern of repeatedly trying to rid himself of those feelings.

What better place to flee for a sense of wholeness and grace than the church? Mike was a good public speaker, had a bright mind, and was well liked by others. He could clear his deep wounding by setting out on a legitimate path that included marriage, the church, and a family of his own. But Mike had a lasting, unhealed problem. He remained conflicted about his sexual urges and was overwhelmed by his own desires. He was in a conflict between his sexual drive and the shame he felt for having it. Without understanding what he was doing, he tried to heal this conflict by having relationships with women who could affirm his sexual pleasures. He rebelled against the inner voices of his mother and father's repression by engaging in affairs with more and more women. This created more shame, and the cycle kept repeating itself.

When the word leaked out about Mike's affairs, the regional minister moved him to another church. He had marital therapy, he grieved, and he moved on. But every Sunday Mike's shame was reinforced by his role as parish pastor. The narcissistic character he portrayed was capable, funny, and strong. Underneath it all, however, Mike felt ashamed of himself. He felt the church members would surely condemn him "if they only knew." He wanted to deal with his sexual shame. He wanted to claim that sex was good and that he was also frightened by it. But he knew the "no talk" rule, and so he remained silent.

Mike was unconsciously trying to rid himself of the shame by reengaging in taboo experience and hoping to feel differently about himself. He was unconsciously reliving his mother's exposure and shame in order to rid himself of it. It was an incurable sexual addiction. Mike was a shame-bound man in a shame-bound system.

Clergy who are ashamed have inner wounds that are so painful that a cloak of acceptable personality is developed for protection. The narcissist has a wounded inner space that he or she covers with a self-confident, charming, seductive exterior. The narcissist falls in love with his or her own image but lacks the ability to be empathetic with himself or herself and therefore with others.

Individuals who feel shame and unworthiness often develop characteristics of narcissism, including a grandiose self-image and a lack of feeling, sense of self, or contact with reality. The narcissistic pastor develops an external presentation that is slick, warm, gregarious, and in essence false. He or she lives in a place of shame that likely affects the faith community. Clergy who are troubled with sexual shame are rarely healed in congregations where silence reigns over all sexual issues.

Congregations and Sexual Secrets

A shame-bound pastoral leader has an exterior that others experience intuitively when coming in contact with the organization. Overt conversations about real issues are impossible because of the threat that the image of the organization (the external "self") would crumble. He can't say openly that he has problems, that he is a sexual person. She can't confess that she has made mistakes, that she has behaved poorly toward others, without her entire image faltering. Congregations may, in fact, attract narcissistic pastors. The pastors' desire to be forgiven and offered grace for some deep internal wounds from childhood compels them to see the church as the family they never had. Unfortunately, congregations have their own tendencies toward the false exterior. Most often faith communities provide a place to continue to hide sexual pain rather than relieve it. Secrets and shame continue under the surface. Congregations whose leaders have been found to have affairs during their leadership of the congregation are bound with sexual secrets and shame. A congregational system is wounded by affairs just as family systems are.

When Sandy arrived at her new parish, the congregation seemed sullen and untalkative. On her first Sunday in worship, a woman stood up during prayer and announced that the reason the last pastor had been moved is that he had had an affair with her. Shocked and horrified, members of the congregation found themselves unmasking the narcissism that led to this betrayal. The congregation was nearly consumed for two years with the healing process that followed. Their use of outside consultants from the counseling community helped move them forward. Had they decided not to talk about it, from that moment on they would have been shame-bound.

Both the sexual health of the congregation and the sexual health of clergy are crucial. Rabbi Edwin Friedman's model of health for congregational life presents the clergyperson as a non-anxious leader.[3] But his model does not fully address sexual anxiety. Sex is a main source of the drive toward power and dominance in all individuals. It involves the tension between individuality and fusion. All relationships have sexual and erotic components. We need to recognize this phenomenon, name it, and deal with it directly within congregational life. Clergy who lead with sexual shame may project it onto others in the shame-to-blame pattern described previously. These leaders will be unlikely to help parishioners who seek healing for their own sexual issues.

The individual who is shame-bound may be repeating the behavior to relieve the anxiety of the taboo. The behavior is tried again in hopes that it will not produce the same feelings another time. The perpetrator of misconduct unconsciously repeats the pattern until it frees him or her from the trap of shame, or until he or she is caught. The resulting shame will confirm his or her deep feelings of unworthiness. In the church this often involves uncovering a narcissistic wound. A pastor who had been hiding his sexual addiction for many years told his therapist, "I know if they discover who

I really am, they will find me as disgusting as I find myself." His deep inner wounds had been hidden by his public persona, but they emerged in his damaging behavior. His sexual misconduct actually served to expose his wounds. In this way he exposed his shame and confirmed his own opinion that he was unredeemable.

The ideal of being a pastoral leader sets the stage for shame. Psychoanalysis describes the ego and the ego ideal as two functioning parts of our lives. For our purposes, I will use the real and ideal self in talking about persons and systems that are shame-bound. The ideal self and the conscience are not really the same. The conscience serves to remind us of wrongdoing and is the place where guilt can be reparative. It invites confession and opens the door for forgiveness and growth. But those who fail to live up to the ideal self live in shame, which is not growth producing.

John Berecz and Herbert Helm Jr. note:

> It is precisely here that we have possibly produced more problems than we have healed because much Christian preaching, writing, and dogma are concerned with raising the ideal self to even higher levels. Unfortunately, this further increases the disparity between the real and ideal selves, producing more shame. The irony is that by attempting to produce better, kinder, purer people, the Christian church has produced more shameful people.[4]

Clergy are extremely susceptible to a disparity between the real and ideal self. The greater the ideal of a Christian leader, the greater the shame for the one who sees him or herself as not meeting the ideal.

After repeated incidents of sexual secrets, a congregation, like an individual, can become entirely overwhelmed with shame. The shame of the leader infects the whole body of Christ with a heavy sense of moral failure, whose powerlessness can become chronic. No matter what the members say or do, they feel as if the congregation is clouded with stigma. And like the victims of family physical or sexual abuse, they feel that they are all shamed and violated.

In order to heal this tendency toward a separation between the idealized and actual sexual self, clergy and congregations will need to address sexual issues openly. Theological education could advance healing in this area through education and psychotherapy for clergy in preparation for their leadership in the parish. A curriculum on human sexuality is crucial to helping new pastors land on solid ground in congregations that are struggling with these issues today. Mandated continuing sexual education for ongoing pastoral leaders, both clergy and lay, is a first step in breaking out of silence on these issues. Whom can clergy trust to discuss these issues without fear of repercussions? Pastoral counselors in each area, denomination, or conference could be instrumental in addressing narcissism and the individual sexual shame that often lies underneath it.

Questions for Reflection

1. Why do you think the church might attract people who are covering up their feelings of unworthiness?
2. Did the story of Mike lead you to think about an awkward moment in your family around some aspect of sexuality?
3. Why do you think that Christianity has historically rejected masturbation?
4. Why are most people anxious about sex?
5. What does your congregation or denomination do to train clergy to understand sexual issues?

9. Individual Shame and the Congregation

Church leaders have become more and more aware that individuals in congregations act out unfinished issues from their families of origin. Author and rabbi Edwin H. Friedman made this phenomenon very clear in his seminal work, *Generation to Generation: Family Process in Church and Synagogue*. He notes that "many of the issues that plague contemporary synagogues and churches are the result of intensified relationships in the nuclear systems of member families (or clergy) when individuals try to substitute their religious organizations for their extended families."[1]

When individuals grow up with family secrets and sexual shame, they seek organizations that are familiar. Some of them look for places that will keep their family secrets intact. Others look for places where healing can begin with more open discussion. Still others seek a grace-filled place that will heal their feelings of shame. Most congregations abound with secrets and plenty of sexual shame. Those who have grown up in similar environments feel at home in those congregations that have secrets and shame.

Secrets in the Church Family

So what happens when the church family begins talking about sexuality? All of those who have personal sexual secrets begin to feel threatened. Those who are unclear about their own sexuality, either in its expression or orientation, begin to feel uneasy with a congregation that opens up the subject. Those who feel they have violated an unspoken sexual rule of the church or of their faith will begin to experience discomfort. Those who are loyal to family secrets that involve sexual shame begin to feel dis-eased as well.

It should not surprise us that talking openly about sexual issues can elicit extremely strong feelings. Not only are those who do the talking suddenly exposed, but those who are silent also feel themselves at risk of exposure. When individuals have internal issues of shame about their own sexuality or sexual past, they will bring this into their interaction with others in the congregation. They often do not have the ability to keep a distance between themselves and the subject. The sexually wounded are vulnerable to any discussion that can open up the wound again. Unlike healthy individuals, the sexually shamed may have lost the ability to empathize with persons who are sexually different or sexually wounded. The inner sexual alienation of the shamed individual will affect relationships at home and in the congregation.

Many a congregation has opened up the topic of homosexuality without a clear idea as to the huge layers of sexual shame that may be unleashed by these discussions. Perhaps a church member comes out of the closet, or maybe a lesbian couple arrives and asks to join the choir. A grieving mother who has lost her son to AIDS asks for prayers for his lover in the worship service. In these circumstances the floodgates of sexual shame open up.

A pastor whose congregation nearly divided over the celebration of a holy union service was said to remark that without exception, each family that left the church or protested the service had an unacknowledged gay or lesbian family member. The daughter of one older couple who were threatening and hostile over the issue came into the pastor's office to confess the family secret of her brother's homosexuality and his parents' shaming of him. A young man from another disgruntled family was seen at a local hamburger joint with his partner. One woman had spoken up loudly against the inclusion of gay people in the life of the church; when she lay dying, the pastor realized that it was time to call the children. Three out of four of them were called. He knew immediately that the fourth one, a daughter living away from the area, was shunned because of her sexual orientation. With much encouragement from friends, the husband invited her home for her mother's last days. It was the first time mother and daughter had seen each other in more than twenty years.

These are but a few examples of the way that personal and familial shame is transferred into the life of the congregation. Without ever naming the reasons for their protest of a holy union or their position on homosexuality, church members often seek to harm the pastor or church leaders who bring the topic into the open.

When a beloved pastor is suddenly bad-mouthed by a handful of people within the congregation, you can bet that there is an underlying issue of shame. Whether the focus is on the pastor, pastoral leadership, or the congregation, issues that are named are often not the core issues. Individual sexual shame is likely the destructive force in the entire system. One person who feels deeply unworthy and comes to the church looking for healing without responsibility or honest confession can distract the entire community from its mission and purpose.

One Man's Search for Wholeness

A therapist received a referral for a new client. The man was talking rapidly and experiencing symptoms of panic. He said that he had to talk to someone in confidence and it needed to be soon. The man was visibly shaking when he sat down in the therapist's office. His palms were wringing wet. He began by saying that he was appalled to learn that two new members of his mostly conservative congregation were gay men. They had become members the previous Sunday. He was outraged that the pastor allowed them to become members of the church. He was sure that their sins were a great weight on God's heart.

The therapist began to intuit that there was a deeper story. She asked, "If you weren't so angry, how would you feel?" He began to sob.

When his sobbing ended, he slowly unraveled the story. It began during his career in the military. He had been on night watch when he heard noises and thought that someone was being hurt. He went around the corner to find two men having sex by the side of the building. They recognized him at once. They were both married men, and they were his superior officers. They turned on him instantly. They threatened him, saying that they would turn him in for homosexual behavior if he ever uttered one word of it, and then they beat him up and left him lying there.

After a lengthy hospitalization, the military moved him to a different company. The entire incident was covered up, and his perpetrators were never reprimanded. He said it was a blessing to have been simply and quietly moved to another location. He wanted to forget the whole thing. He did this successfully until the Sunday when two gay men stood at the altar before God and the church and were blessed as members of the fellowship.

His church pastor's decision to welcome the men thrust this scene back into his memory with a huge weight of shame and pain. He carried embarrassment and disgust about himself and the incident, even though he had successfully repressed the memories. When his pain reemerged he could no longer keep the secret.

Telling the story produced relief, but it didn't fully relieve him of his feelings of shame.

He found himself confused and disgusted by homosexual behavior and unable to separate it from the violence of his assault. What they did to him was so wrong that he had concluded that all sex between men was morally repugnant. The task of his work in counseling was first to separate his witnessing the act from feeling that he had some involvement in it. His next steps in healing involved a peeling apart of sexuality and sexual violence. Once he could recognize that his assault was not about homosexual consensual sex but was an act of violence, his healing could progress. When the men turned on him, they did so to assert their power and control over him, not for sexual gratification. This aspect of the healing is difficult for anyone who has been sexually assaulted. The lines between sexual behavior and assault can get blurry. The shame of the violence and the shame of the sexual act associated with it more than doubles; it multiplies the sense of unworthiness that victims feel.

While the man sought healing with a pastoral counselor, he could not do so in the congregation. He felt that the direction the church was taking was also a violation of his beliefs about gay people and a violation of his own integrity. His pastor and his congregation would never learn why he left the church. There was no opportunity for people to talk about such experiences. No mention had ever been made about sexual violence and the grace of God that can restore wholeness. He chose simply to leave the church and look for another congregation that espoused the belief that homosexuality is a sin, so that the issues of his own assault could be avoided.

This man's story illustrates the explosive dynamics that may result from conversations about sexuality in the church. So many of us are wounded sexually that any mention of the topic can lead to re-wounding the individuals in the church. Only through careful acknowledgment of the many sexual wounds that people have suffered will these conversations feel safe for victims of assault. With tremendous love and compassion for all who are sexually wounded, faith communities will move from places of reinjury toward becoming places of healing.

Questions for Reflection

1. Do you know people who have come to the church to be healed of their sexual past?
2. Only if it feels entirely safe to do so, discuss an area of sexual healing that you would like for yourself or someone in your family.
3. How has your church opened up the subject of homosexuality?
4. How have you felt about your church's conversations about sexuality?
5. Are congregational leaders prone to shame or grace or a little of both?

10. The Rules

In most family systems, rules establish the boundaries for shame. There are many parallels between families and congregations in patterns of behavior and functioning.[1] In this chapter I examine and illustrate the ways that church families have rules related to shame that operate like the rules in nuclear families.[2] In families and congregational families there are many unspoken rules. Where shame operates: 1) you don't know what the rules are; 2) there are plenty of rules, but no one names them; 3) you'll know you've broken the rules by the shame you receive; 4) the rules don't apply to everyone in the same way; 5) if you break the rules, you are unworthy to receive forgiveness; and 6) no one talks *openly* about breaking the rules.

1. You don't know what the rules are.

Shame-bound families are prone to have a great deal of confusion about the rules. What are the rules? Who interprets them? Who enforces them and why? Can we talk about them? If not, why not?

In most congregational families the big book of rules is the Bible. This can be a source of confusion. Biblical issues having to do with human sexuality are conflicted, are debated by scholarship, and appear outdated in an age of sexual freedom. Yet many congregational families turn to the text and focus on the prohibitions of Scripture. Sexual behaviors from bestiality to dishonoring the temple of the body are included in the book of Leviticus and in Paul's writings. Some of the rules are spoken of frequently, while others are overlooked. Some significant scriptural rules about sexuality are ignored entirely. For example, not many sermons are preached about abstaining from sex with a woman who is menstruating. Not many preachers have decried King David's rule-breaking relationship with Bathsheba. Incest and the sexual exploitation of children are rarely elaborated upon. The list of prohibitions includes words that have no direct translation from Hebrew and Greek concepts into contemporary English. The translation of words like *malokos,* which means literally "the soft," into "the effeminate" or "homosexual" has scholars scrambling to locate the actual meaning of the rule.[3] The rule about not "lusting" in the heart was mocked by the media during President Carter's years in office and is often preached about in congregations. Why was there a stunned silence from many church pulpits in the face of a Christian president's (Clinton's) sexual misconduct? We have so little experience talking about the gray areas regarding sexual behavior that we are ill prepared to respond ethically. If we remain fixated on selective biblical mandates, we reinforce shame about rule breaking.

In each generation, biblical interpreters set the texts into the context of their own sexual ethics. The rules appear to be changing from time to time, which is even more confusing. The term for sexual perverts, for example, is highly unclear. The root word *malokos* was not interpreted to mean homosexuality by the early Christian commentators, since it means "softness" in its literal form. Other sexual prohibitions include "sin against your own body" (1 Cor. 6:18): Do not rule over the body of someone else, and maintain self-control. This list has been interpreted and reinterpreted by every generation.

In congregational families in which shame operates, there is no allowance for variance in the rules. There is rarely an admission that the rules contradict themselves. In shame-bound families everyone is just expected to know what the rules are and to follow them. Not too many Sunday school teachers have put these lists of sexual rules on the blackboard and explained them.

2. There are plenty of rules, but no one names them.
When I ask people what they learned in church about sex, they never name any concrete rules. They say things like: "I learned to sit with my knees together," or "I learned that Mary was a virgin and that's why I should be one too." People learn a lot about sex in church without ever actually being taught about it. It's the unspoken messages that come through. The Bible isn't often used to teach children and adolescents about sex. When it comes to sexuality, the standards of the church are made evident in many indirect ways, and the process is often arbitrary.

When the rules aren't clear to everyone, the shaming that results is based on more than disobedience to a tradition or biblical edict. By not clarifying the rules, sentences can be handed out at the discretion of the pastor or church leaders. Shame is more likely to fall on the newcomer, the adolescent, the woman, and the gay person. The sexual indiscretion of the adulterous elder is overlooked, while the suggestion of a public demonstration of new love on the part of a young divorcée is punished severely. A young woman who is pregnant is shunned, but the young man who impregnates her remains protected by anonymity. The young are chastised for sexually overt music and videos, while their fathers spend time in Internet sex chat rooms.

In this complex day the church needs to become very conscious of unspoken rules. The danger of not being clear about the rules is that those in charge get to determine them incident by incident. This is a less than satisfactory solution.

3. You'll know you've broken the rules by the shame you receive.

In shame-bound systems the rules become evident not through open discussion but through the subsequent punishments. When a young man I'll call "Jack" began dating a woman from his church, everyone was pleased. When the elders learned that the two of them had gone on a week-long vacation together, they shunned and banished the couple from the congregation. Months earlier when Jack joined the church, no one had said anything to him about rules for singles. But as soon as he violated a rule, he was stigmatized. A few men of the board of elders came to his house one evening to tell him that he didn't belong in the church any longer. Jack left the congregation feeling angry and resentful. The congregational family had waited until he had violated their sexual values to explain them. By then Jack was "unworthy" to remain in the church family. "In shame-bound systems the children are not told clearly what is expected of them but they are a constant disappointment."[4]

At a California church that I served as pastor, we were blessed by a vanload of young adults from a nearby group home who began coming to worship. To this day I don't know how or why they picked our congregation, but they did. Ricky was in a wheelchair. Walt wore a crash helmet on his head so that when he had seizures he wouldn't be injured. Kate appeared to be just fine, yet her speech was slow and she sometimes stopped mid-sentence and changed the subject. They were very warm and friendly.

It just so happened that these three folks caused a major upheaval in the life of the church. Whenever I asked a question in the midst of my sermon, Kate would answer it. She had not learned to distinguish between the rhetorical question and the real question. In some worship cultures this would have been expected of the congregation, but in our silent, mostly Euro-Caucasian congregation this violated a taboo. Walt would get up from church at various times during the worship hour to use the bathroom. Kate, sensing that this was okay, began to do that too. They sat in the front row, and several times in the hour they would come and go, no matter the place we were in the order of worship.

A growing number of church leaders were uncomfortable with the behavior of these new participants. The worship committee planned to discuss the matter at their next meeting. They wanted to know what to do because the new visitors were violating the rules. Their speech was loaded with unconscious stigma and shame toward the young people, evidenced by the use of "they should" and "like everybody else." And the word *rules* came up. I let board members speak their piece and then asked, "The rules?" They were quiet. "What are the rules? Maybe I don't know them either."

As it turned out, they had a set of unspoken rules. The more we talked about them, the more we found ourselves in disagreement. Do we allow kissing and hugging in worship? Is it okay to get up to use the bathroom during the reading of the Scripture lessons?

At first, several members of the governing board were insistent that I go to the group home of our visitors and tell them that they can't do this, that, and the other. I resisted, refusing to go until I could tell them what they *could* do as well as what they couldn't do. And if I was going to tell them not to get up at the time of the Gospel reading, I wanted to explain this rule in the context of how sacred the Gospel reading is to us and why.

The board began to play with the question of cultural norms. We developed a lighthearted questionnaire about what you can and can't do in church. Surprisingly, a lot more people said it is okay to kiss in church than I ever expected. Holding hands was fine too. At the offering time it was deemed okay to tear checks out of your checkbook. Together we shaped a common language for what we hoped the worship environment would be like and became conscious of why we wanted it that way. Then we agreed to use the worship service as a teaching moment for everyone about the survey results and reasons for our norms in worship. In this way we never singled out anyone for violating an unstated rule. No one was shamed, and everyone was included. We had changed a situation of shame into a situation of grace.

4. The rules don't apply to everyone equally.

In the area of human sexual behavior, rules are essential. They serve to keep us in loving covenants and out of physical and psychic danger. We need rules for human sexual behavior because people are exploited for money, personal narcissistic gratification, power and intimidation, and sexual violence. Children need to be protected, and the powerless need to be affirmed and uplifted. The boundaries prevent the degradation of another for sexual pleasure that can result in lifelong psychological and spiritual illness.

Sexual rules are crucial as they define loving behavior and exploitative immoral behavior. The rule of fidelity protects the couple from the confusion of multiple intimacies and the potential of secrets and betrayals. In healthy families and in healthy congregational families, the rules are made clear, are discussed, and are more than strict sets of behavioral guidelines. They become ethical guidelines, not just a list of shoulds and don'ts. In families in which there is shame, however, sexuality is suspect and behaviors are rule-bound.

Today churches are being shaken by huge challenges to traditional sexual rules. The rules today are confused by the interface with marriage as legalized by the state. No biblical comments on marriage can be directly translated into what couples do at the county clerk's office when they fill out the license-request form. Unmarried partners are challenging the church's presumption that only state-sanctioned, legalized marriage is ethically viable. Gay and lesbian couples are challenging the courts to define marriage as a legal contract to ensure benefits, and they are challenging the church to honor and sanctify their promises of sexual fidelity.

Church history shows a precedent in this area. An entire history of same-sex unions in the church and around the world is available in the work of John Boswell.[5] Legalized marriage wasn't even connected to services in the church throughout most of Christian history. Marriage was seen as an act wherein two people proclaimed their faithfulness in the sight of God. In biblical times marriage rules served to ensure that no one violated anyone else's property. Marriage was seen, as far back as St. Paul, as the way to deal with sexual tension. And Jesus blessed a wedding at Cana as the first sign of his miraculous ministry.

Many would agree that it is the job of the family and the church family to help individuals define Christlike love and to set boundaries that ensure faithful, loving sexual relationships. The church has placed its focus on the institution of marriage while at the same time avoiding discussion of the range of human sexual behavior and orientation. We have talked about sex rules without actually talking about sex.

An entire book could be written about the church's involvement in legal and covenantal marriages. What many leaders are now saying is that the church has a commitment to covenant-making. With regard to sexuality the church needs to take a clear and forthright stand on fidelity in relationships. It has not consistently done so. The media have mocked the church for its "holier-than-thou" preaching while at the same time keeping silent about its leaders' adulterous affairs. The church has been seen as a place of extreme hypocrisy because it has been silent and complacent about the indiscretions of its leaders while shaming those who choose faithfulness without the legality of marriage. In so doing the church is acting like a family steeped in shame. The rules are not applied equally.

5. You can't confess and receive forgiveness because you are unworthy.

In a healthy system the violation of one's own or the organization's values produces guilt. Remember, guilt is the moral voice that says, "I've done something that hurt me or someone else; I will need to make a change." Guilt is the moral conscious based on a specific behavior that can be amended by confession or apology. It serves a preventative function, keeping one aware of the damages of another lapse in behavior.

A client grew up with parents who never affirmed him. He was always in trouble, and he was always to blame. When he recently faced an area in his marriage in which he and his wife both clearly thought that he had been out of line, he talked about his remorse, but he didn't know what to do next. It was his family pattern to grovel in his own unworthiness. When I asked if he had ever considered an apology, he laughed and said, "I've never seen anyone do that!" I was stunned. "No one, not a friend, or sibling, or someone at the office?" He maintained that he had never witnessed or experienced the process of asking for and receiving forgiveness. The shame in his family and in his self-image was very deep.

In a family steeped in shame one is never forgiven. Jack, the man who invited the single woman to vacation with him, learned from the attitude of the elders that he would never be forgiven. So his only option was to leave the family.

A young woman's pregnancy became the source of ongoing sexual shame in another parish. When she was in her teens she became pregnant "out of wedlock," as the elders put it. The sideways glances and the downcast eyes told her that the community no longer accepted her. How could she, in this instance, ask for and receive their forgiveness? The elders tolerated her because of her parents, who were active in the congregation. But their previous outspoken love had turned to shame, and tolerance was all they offered her after that. She was not invited to participate in any functions except worship. When she volunteered to teach Sunday school several years later, they still spoke of her behind her back. When she came to a meeting a few minutes late, it was as if she had betrayed the family all over again. To hear them talk about her, even a stranger would guess that there was something behind their comments.

No words were ever directly spoken, but she could feel their judgment. She knew it through their nonverbal language and shifting of alliances and friendships in the church. When the annual shower for all of the new mothers took place, she was not invited. Hers was the only child born that year who did not receive the little knitted booties that the women's guild had labored over for weeks. The other parents received gifts like layettes and strollers. She was given nothing. This pain deeply wounded her and left the entire church family embarrassed. Her church family shunned and shamed her. Those who reflected on the incident years later finally began to name and confess their own shaming behavior toward her. And only at that point could everyone begin to move toward confession and forgiveness.

6. No one talks openly about violations, but everybody gossips about them.

Media attention and litigation surrounding clergy sexual misconduct have raised awareness about the sexual sins of clergy. As moral leaders, sexual indiscretions result in damage to individual victims, loss of respect for the profession, and loss of faith in the system in which the rules operate. The tendency of the church to cover up sexual harassment, misconduct, and violations of fidelity norms has increased the church's shame. If the perpetrator, the victim, or the congregation is shame-bound, it takes a great deal of careful recovery to feel good again. The guilt about the behavior is unpardonable. Entire congregations can be emotionally overtaken by the deep unworthiness and embarrassment known as shame. Within congregations the indiscretions of clergy leaders are gossiped about but rarely dealt with openly.

In one parish the congregation was locked in shame by a secret about their former pastor. He was a single man and had an out-of-town girlfriend, who was a member of his former congregation. She came to town and stayed at the parsonage on occasional weekends. Most people knew about the situation, but no one talked openly about it. Many people felt this to be a violation of their Christian values, and they could never respect the man as a spiritual model. Rather than address the tension openly, they wrote letters to the bishop asking that the pastor be reassigned. They concocted a great number of problems about his personality and leadership style in order to justify his relocation. His leaving never resolved the issue.

When the next pastor arrived, also a single man, all of the congregation's unfinished business about sexuality and singleness was under the table. On top of the table, the people seemed unwilling to grant the new pastor any authority, and they tightly controlled discussions based on who was "in the know" and who was not. Judgment and anger transferred from the first pastor to the second one within the unconscious of the community. The new pastor's ability to lead the church was diminished by an old cloud of suspicion and resentment.

An organization masks its unspoken shame in many different ways. It may appear to be rigid, while its rigidity is simply an attempt to avoid addressing the emotional (affective) states of the family system. Unspoken shame covers tightly controlled anger, which, when repressed, can be intuited by the newcomer.

Until the violation of this congregation's rules could be addressed, healing was impossible. New people found it hard to fit in, and those "gut feelings" that people have when something is wrong were felt in worship and fellowship times alike. The tendency of this congregation to point fingers, place blame, and gossip behind people's backs had initiated a decline that needed serious intervention and healing.

Christians who believe strongly that you should not talk about sex end up fighting about it instead. A regional conference of the United Methodist Church has recently been consumed with the debate over conducting holy union services, which are similar to weddings, for same-sex couples. By a decision of the highest court of the national church and a rule in the church's "Social Principles" section of the *Book of Discipline,* holy unions are prohibited. Seventeen churches in disagreement with the conference's liberal trend toward the open acceptance of gay people have threatened to leave the conference.

In the midst of threatened losses of churches and clergy, conference leaders devised a plan to provide meetings in which people could talk to one another about the issues that were dividing them. A consultant was hired, and a series of listening sessions were held. In these sessions clergy were asked to name the "elephants" in the church family. The term *elephants* is often used to refer to something in a family system that everyone knows about but no one talks about. In the alcoholic family, for example, the fact that Mom drinks is never mentioned, but the secret is the "elephant in the living room."

The discussions took place over several months at locations throughout the conference. The "elephants" that clergy named were listed on paper, prioritized, and acknowledged. In the majority of cases the clergy listed "biblical authority" or "how we interpret the Bible" as the largest area of problem or disagreement. But the consultant found that in every case the real issue underlying it all was sexuality. The clergy couldn't *say* that they wanted to talk about sex. They certainly couldn't *say* that they wanted to talk about homosexuality. But it was, in fact, what they talked about both inside of the meeting and outside of it.

Summarizing the Rules

The rules of family and church family shame are complex. They involve the rule setters and the rule violators. The "no talk" rule about sex in most families is alive and operative in congregations with an underlying layer of permission for gossip, cover-ups, and blame. Those in power often live with a different set of rules from those who are new or different. The adulterer sits in judgment of the gay person. The pastor who attempts to seduce a parishioner is moved to another location without disclosure. The sexual rules apply to some and not to others, and the Bible is used to justify several different positions. It is no wonder that many former members of congregations are now in exile.

A woman who is healing from three generations of incest described her inability to remain in her congregation. When she learned that her husband, an elder of good standing in the church, was molesting their teenaged daughter, she notified the police. His subsequent arrest and imprisonment shocked the community. She needed the support of her congregation as did her daughter, and instead found that she was criticized and shunned. How dare she? Not only had her husband been an elder, but his father was also a respected man in the church and community. The fact that they both had a history of child sexual assault was entirely forgiven by the powers of the church. The church was ashamed that she had exposed them. She had blown the whistle on generations of perpetrators who had found safety in the congregation. Rather than face their part in covering up for the sins of the church "fathers," they made it too uncomfortable for her to stay. The truth around sexual deviance is not often appreciated. The telling of it, however, is essential for the healing of victims and coconspirators.

The trouble with church rules about sexuality is the arbitrary way in which they are applied. Whom do they nail, and who avoids them? Who establishes them, and who may change them? Are the people with the most power exempt? Sexuality that is denied and repressed by the "no talking" rule will not be relegated to the secular culture. One's spiritual self and one's sexual self cannot be separated without the danger of shame and violence. Carl Jung once remarked that when people brought sexual questions to him they invariably turned out to be religious questions, and when they brought religious questions to him they always turned out to be sexual ones.[6]

Questions for Reflection

1. What "no talk" rules operate or operated in your family of origin, in your family now, and in your congregation?
2. The author seems to suggest that these rules do more harm than good. What do you think?
3. Discuss a situation in which you learned of the rules after you had broken them.
4. Is there a time in your life when you were surprised to be forgiven?
5. What "unforgivable sins" might lead to shame in your faith community?
6. How does gossip increase shame?
7. Can you think of a time when it seemed as if the rules didn't apply to someone in power?
8. Do the rules in your congregation apply to everyone in the same way?

11. Sexual Identity Shame

One Who Returned to Give Thanks

After a funeral service I went to my office to check my in-box for mail and assorted phone memos. I lost track of the time. When I next looked across the lawn, I saw, with panic, that no one was there. The mourners who had been talking had all left for the burial site and would be waiting for me. I grabbed my jacket and dashed into the sanctuary to retrieve my service notes from the pulpit.

A young man was kneeling at the communion rail directly below the pulpit, where my notes rested. Was he with the family? He didn't appear to be a transient hoping for a handout. I had not seen him before.

I slowed down, excused myself for disturbing his prayer, and stepped past him up to the pulpit and grabbed my notes. When I turned to descend, the man had risen and was blocking my escape.

"Where can I find the pastor?" he asked.

"You've found her," I said, wondering what was next.

"That's great." He brightened. "I'm glad there's a woman here now. This church is finally progressing. I was active in the youth group here when I was in high school. If it weren't for that group I don't think I'd believe in God today. It meant a lot to me."

He paused, then said, "I have AIDS. I'm dying."

I wondered how many times he had reported his own death sentence. He spoke of it without resignation or resentment.

"I want to give you something," he said. He slipped a diamond ring off of his finger and held it out for me to get a closer look. He described it in detail: the art deco style, the cut of the gem, how much he'd been told it was worth. He placed the ring in my hand. "I want you to get the best price you can for it and use it for your youth ministry."

A dying man had dropped by to bless the church. In the middle of a service honoring the dead, here was a living witness to the power of faith and hope. I wanted to linger in the moment. I wanted to hear his story.

"Could we meet here in half an hour? I have a graveside service I have to get to."

"No," he said. "I can't stay long; I'm just passing through. I only came to pray and to give you the ring."

"Do you belong to a church that will help you through this?" I asked.

"No, but I have a great group of friends."

He reached out, embraced me, and turned to go. I stood for a moment on the steps unable to move. I called after him: "I didn't get your name." He said, "Let's keep it anonymous." He paused to take in the space of the sanctuary, a last good-bye. When he set off down the aisle to the front door, I went out the side door.

The ministry of the church was in this young man's heart at the time of his death. The church had given him a faith he surely needed to face his own death. I never learned who his youth leader had been or what called him back. How had that person succeeded in gifting this man with Jesus to lean upon?

But I also cannot help wondering if the church's acceptance of him in his early teens might have prevented his eventual diagnosis. When the AIDS epidemic was first uncovered, Christians quoted by the media were saying that AIDS was a curse from God. Many people, already sure of their eternal damnation, threw caution to the wind and acted out. Sexual experimentation and exploitation result from a lack of spirituality in sexuality. Did his spirituality include a shame-free acceptance of his own sexual orientation? Or was he, like millions of others, burdened down by the messages he received in places of faith?

I don't think that the church of the seventies and eighties would have talked with him about sexual desire and sexual safety. It wouldn't have allowed for a gay identity. I began thinking about his family. Were they still in the congregation? Would they have the courage to tell others that their gay son is dying? Did the congregation's love of all people prepare his parents to welcome him home or to reject him for his "immorality"?

How often I have heard a church member say, "We don't have any homosexuals in our church." Of course, those who are there are likely to be silent about it. Or they have left the church so that they might free themselves from shame.

Sexual Identity Shame

Sexual identity shame is the result of the religious oppression of sexual minorities. Both the gay person and his or her family find

their life in the church to be precarious at best and painfully abusive at worst. Religious shaming of gay people not only underlies
exclusionary practices but, taken to the extreme, leads to hate
crimes. Sexual orientation shame leads to the invalidation of people, the discounting of them, the objectifying of them as if they
were not fully human and sacred. These attitudes lead to gay
bashing and murder. A man who was arrested in a string of gay
bashings told a reporter that he did it because his father had
repeatedly taunted him with threats and called him "a little fag-
got." His own fear that he was possibly gay was so threatening to
him that he began ridding himself of it by violent acts toward gay
men in his community.

The shaming of gay people is a significant roadblock to mental
and spiritual health. Psychologist Joseph Neisen writes about the
healing necessary to recover from what he calls "shame due to heterosexism." He illustrates the way culture, strongly supported by
lessons of the Judeo-Christian tradition, perpetuates prejudice by
discrimination. The most pernicious attitude is that there is no such
thing as a gay, lesbian, or bisexual orientation. He explains that
individuals within a victimized minority learn at an early age to
devalue themselves and to honor those persons in the majority as
superior: "The impact of heterosexism on gays/lesbians/bisexuals
in today's society is in hampering individual growth and development by instilling shame. . . . Oppression contributes to the shame
many individuals within the victimized minority feel."[1]

Neisen goes on to parallel the experience of gays, lesbians, and
bisexuals with the experience of other victimized people, who also
become convinced that the problem is who they are rather than the
oppression of the culture. The effects of sexual shame through sexual victimization are similar to the effects of sexual shame on gays,
lesbians, and bisexuals. They develop the thoughts of their oppres-
sors by thinking that perhaps the abuse is deserved. The gay adolescent might say, "Maybe gay people *are* sick, and I deserve to be
put down, beat up, shunned." The person who is victimized says
things like, "I'm dirty for having participated in that sexual act," or
"I'm bad, otherwise he might not have done that to me." And: "No
one will love me because I'm damaged." The gay person who is
trying to affirm him or herself will echo these statements. He or she
will draw conclusions from the surrounding culture. It doesn't take
too many negative labeling experiences before someone concludes,
"I'm bad for acting on my homosexual desires," and "No one will
love me because I'm gay—especially my friends and family."

Such feelings reduce people to a place of intense powerlessness and mistrust. They feel the need to keep their secret to themselves, and they live in fear of being found out. Again, Neisen reports:

> After years of growing up hearing negative messages about homosexuality from heterosexist individuals and institutions, gay and lesbian individuals undoubtedly internalize some of these messages and begin to believe, "there is something wrong with me for being gay/lesbian," "I am bad," "I am unworthy," "I am sick," "I am unlovable," and "I am going to hell because I am gay." Whenever . . . society instills these myths and negative stereotypes in young minds it commits a form of abuse with harmful consequences similar to those resulting from sexual or physical abuse.[2]

The Isolation of Shame

Gays, lesbians, bisexuals, and their families commonly feel extremely isolated from God and from congregations wherein they fear they will hear exclusionary and oppressive comments about them. Whether it is the overt shaming by well-intentioned Christians or the derogatory jokes that can still be overheard at potlucks, gay people struggle to maintain a sense of dignity in the face of the shaming by most congregations. When all relationships are described as male-female, all partnerships as marriages, all adolescent girls are expected to be "boy crazy" and adolescent boys are supposed to be "girl crazy," the gay individual experiences a searing pang of unworthiness. Even the unspoken silences are felt at a very intuitive level. Many faithful men and women have fled the church to be healed of its shaming.

A lesbian tells her story:

> My mother recently told me that she has prayed for me for over two decades that I would return to the Christian church. I walked away from it when I was seventeen years old. I was a rebellious but philosophical teen, striving to understand myself. The church's teachings about matters of sexuality did not make sense to me. Perhaps I knew subconsciously that there was something different about me. I had been attracted to other girls and grown women since the age of thirteen. I probably sensed that I would not fit into the church's social life or moral code. I knew that I was different from others internally, and that my life would be changed by it. Even before I knew anything about the "coming out" process, I knew that I wouldn't fit into the norm.

It took me ten years after I left the church to finally come out. Between times, in my search for meaning and spirituality, I connected up with a church that had all women ministers, some of whom had homosexual experiences. There were gay men in the church as well. Falling in love with a female friend was what led me to that church. I was comfortable and at home there, but it was not a Christian denomination. According to my mother it was a cult, and although the church celebrated the life of Jesus, it was metaphysical and "new age." I ended up being hurt and disillusioned once again.

When I came out to my mother seventeen years ago, her main comment was that she could accept my homosexuality because she knew that I could be a Christian even though I was a homosexual. She knew this because she had heard of the Metropolitan Community Church. I wasn't lectured or rejected with the use of Christian dogma; instead my mother was just concerned that I would have a Christian home.

I was without a church home for a while. I wanted to be part of a congregation. I could not yet find a place where worship included all of life, God's creation, and spiritual unity. I wasn't content to worship in an isolated denomination, as if gays and lesbians should be segregated, as in some state of imperfection, like a leper's colony. I also recognized that I couldn't celebrate a religion or be part of a church that didn't accept how God made me.

Recently, I have begun attending a church that is "open and affirming." The fact that I'm a lesbian is not something I need to announce about myself. Primarily I feel an acceptance there for all of me. I know that the love I feel in my heart is sacred and that it is not a sin. Being gay is not primary, but it is an important part of my loving and intimate relationships. I am part of a church that honors the love between two people, regardless of gender.

I hope that one day I will be able to be married in a Christian church. I can't imagine attending a church where I wasn't able to receive blessings and enjoy the sacraments like other members. Christianity is for people of all nations, cultures, and races. Jesus was an inclusive leader, and he did not turn people away.

I think about my mother's prayers for me and wonder if her prayers should have been for the Christian church, which could have provided an open door for other gays and me. If there is to be an open heart, there must first be an open door. This is what I found out and I am glad. Within that open door and community, my mother's prayers have, at last, been answered.[3]

Two kinds of shame are described in this woman's story. The first is the external condemnation of the community of faith; the second is the internalized self-condemnation that resulted from it. She needed self-acceptance, which was not possible within the condemnation of the church. She also needed a community of faith in which her sexual self could find grace and acceptance so that she could emerge from shame.[4]

Families Ashamed

The family members of gays, lesbians, bisexuals, and transgendered persons who are open about their loved ones also seek congregations who express acceptance. As the adult child of a gay father, I felt enormous pride walking in the Fourth of July parade with members of Parents, Family, and Friends of Lesbians, Gays, Bisexuals and Transgendered Persons (PFLAG).[5] In many communities this interfaith group provides fellowship within churches so that people can be sure that no one will condemn their loved ones.

Children grow up learning the identity shame that their parents carried. Family shame is an inherited dis-ease. When children learn the internalized homophobia of their parents, they too will find it hard to be in a faith community that sees homosexuality as an abominable sin.[6] My research into the effects on children of growing up in closeted homosexual families indicates that the shaming of the culture is passed to the children in the form of anxiety, fear, and shame.[7]

A woman who learned of my studies in this field recently shared her story. "I want to learn more about your research," Mia said. This beautiful woman in her mid-thirties was looking at the floor. I provided a brief introduction to my work. She kept her eyes cast downward while I spoke. "Why is it an interest of yours?" Silence. I had asked the question too pointedly, too directly. "I haven't told anyone about this," she whispered. I could see that her story had shame attached to it. I honored her pace and knew that it must be profoundly unsettling. "I think that my husband is gay." She was greatly concerned about the effects of his secret on the children. She wanted to know how to cope with it all, how to help him out of the closet if he needed to emerge. She talked about the intense fear of living as a church leader, when at any time the truth could be found out and her family would be ostracized. Looking down to the ground, she was embodying the shame of her husband's ambiguous sexual orientation. She was experiencing a great deal of fear that if the situation were revealed to the local church or to her judicatory that her ministry and her family would be gravely damaged. Mia's situation is not unique. The spouses, the parents, and the children of gay, lesbian, bisexual, and transgendered people take on the shame as if it were their own. They too are often trapped in silence.

Are there signs of hope? With more and more congregations declaring themselves to be accepting, people have more options than they did ten or fifteen years ago. There are AIDS ministries assisting in the support of people like the young man who returned to thank his church. There are PFLAG groups in most areas of the country. The healing has begun. But before we turn to it, we need to take a look at the ways that the specific shaming behaviors of the church around sexuality reflect a broader possibility of the church as a shame-bound culture.

We can't move toward healing until we understand the individual, the family, and the culture in which sexual shame operates. The next chapter will provide evidence that the church has its work cut out for it in beginning to change the culture of shame that has been shaped by its theology, tradition, and history.

Questions for Reflection
1. Discuss with your study group your feelings as you read the story about the man and the ring.
2. Do any people in your congregation have AIDS, or are any HIV-positive? Are there likely some that you would never hear about?
3. Do you agree with the author that heterosexism leads to hate crimes?
4. Could you identify with the mother of the lesbian woman who was searching for a church home? Explain.
5. When sexual shame operates in a family, everyone feels it. Can you think of a time when shame rubbed off on you from someone in your family?
6. Discuss the way that family secrets might increase someone's experience of shame.

12. Shame and Culture

Cultural Shame Theory

We can begin to look at healing the shame that exists in individual lives by placing these experiences in the context of Christian culture. Individual shame is clearly a product of the dominant culture. It is beyond one's own room or the family room that one experiences the motives of shame and honor. These are public encounters. Some particular cultures use shame as their primary mode of operation. Shame enforces the moral agenda. Shame reinforces the norms, values, and beliefs of the culture. Cultures in which repeated shame experiences are dominant are called "shame cultures."

Theorists of shame tell us that shame is the emotion of being watched and is most often found in social experience. Gabriele Taylor writes:

> The person who feels proud needs to be self-conscious in the sense that he must have some awareness of his position in the world, and have some conception of his worth, however inarticulate that might be. The self-consciousness required for shame, however, seems to be of a higher order than this. The person feeling shame feels exposed: he thinks of himself as being seen through the eyes of another. The case of shame introduces an observer or audience.[1]

Those who experience exposure and shame repeatedly develop identities related to the expectation of unworthiness. Taylor makes the point that when persons break the rules of the culture, they experience exposure and shame. Theoretically, all shame has at its core an observer, whether we have internalized the response of the imagined others or are directly shamed by them face-to-face. People who have experienced the shame of the church have an internalized expectation that when walking into a church they will again feel that shame.

In *The Psychology of Shame*, Gershen Kaufman notes:

> The role of culture in molding personality is no less crucial than the role of family or peer group; it is only less visible. Culture is the fabric that bonds a people together . . . a web of

> meaning created out of symbols and traditions. An interpersonal bridge stretches through our cultural consciousness, uniting us in common purpose. The evolution of culture is fueled by the identification need; we feel identified with one another, and thereby experience *communion*."[2] [italics added]

The search for communion is at the core of involvement in religious life. The desire is to be one among many of similar values and to be accepted within the circle. When this does not take place, shame and humiliation become the primary emotional experience. After several experiences of sensing "unworthiness," of lowering one's head for failures—perceived or actual—one begins to live in anticipation that this will be the experience and that the effect of shame is appropriate within the culture.

Kaufman and other shame theorists describe the snowballing effects of shame in individuals, effects that create entire cultures governed by shame. Does the culture of the church (its rituals, beliefs, symbols, and heroes) reinforce the shame affect, or does it liberate members from shame? What are the signs of the church being a shame-based culture?

Social Shame

Describing social shame, Evelyn and James Whitehead look at three behaviors, which they call the "strategies of social shame." They illustrate some key elements of cultural shame. These strategies indicate a shame-based culture. They include naming the person deviant, belittling him or her, and silencing him or her. They write: "Deviant names stigmatize, marking the shamed person as not fitting in, as unworthy of membership in this group. This labeling strategy survives in our religious and political lives."[3]

Are these three strategies active in the church? Certainly members of the gay, lesbian, bisexual, and transgendered community and their loved ones could put together a long list of words the church has used to shun and shame them. Women have experienced name-calling around their sexuality more intensely than men. Terms like *hussy* and *slut* have been spoken from the pulpit. The whispers of those who brand a child "illegitimate" are involved in shaming. The adulterer is branded. A person with questionable morals is "loose" or "easy." These terms abound. The church's use of the term *sinner* is selective. While most Christians would admit that we are all sinners, groups of people and certain individuals are labeled as such.

An illustration of the church as a culture of sexual shame is found in Nathaniel Hawthorne's classic story *The Scarlet Letter*, in which Hester Prynne falls from grace by bearing the illegitimate child of the local clergyman. She is punished by a pronouncement that she must "wear a mark of shame upon her bosom,"[4] the curse of wearing a scarlet letter "A" for her adultery. The community's boundary of sexual behavior was violated, and she paid the price for it in stigma and silencing. In refusing to divulge the name of the child's father, Hester took his shame upon herself and saved the community from the shame of exposure to a fallen pastor. This shame would have placed a shadow on God and their religion itself.

In the 1850s Hester became a symbol of redemption. She transformed her shame by good works, thus turning the symbol of the letter "A" into a beautiful mark. From our modern perspective, however, we know that the church has inherited not only the damage of its own shaming but also the damage of the silence that protected but did not redeem Hester's lover.

Church culture has been particularly vicious in its use of naming to inflict sexual shame. Youths, who are quick to pick up on and use terms found in the dominant culture, have not been given good alternatives. Shaming through labeling (naming) others as "sexually deviant" or "perverted" contributes to the high suicide rates among gay, lesbian, bisexual, and transgendered teens. Many of today's youths feel themselves caught in the extreme polarization of a permissive sexual culture and repressive religious culture. By their teens, youths raised in the culture of the mainline church have learned a great deal about shaming and being shamed.

How is it that the culture of the church creates and repeats scenes of shame in such a way that people end up with "scripts" in which they expect to be shamed within the culture? How is it that they feel they have a right to shame others outside of their own religious beliefs? While my comments are applicable to many religious cultures, here I am focused on the mainline Protestant and Catholic traditions that affect religious beliefs, rituals, and actions in this new millennium. The healing of sexual shame will be possible only with a fuller view of the use of shame to teach, monitor, and correct persons in the faith community.

Several organizing scripts are at work in the shame-bound culture of the church. These scripts are the basis of my assessment that the mainline church is a shame-bound culture. What are these scripts? They are: perfection, self-denial, idealism, gender domination, unworthiness, and condemnation. These are spelled out in Scripture and in the traditions of Christian culture. They are reinforced through rituals, pastoral teaching, social interactions, small groups, and individual relationships.

Perfectionism

> "Be perfect, therefore, as your heavenly Father is perfect."
> (Matt. 5:48)

We have previously spoken of shame as the experience of ourselves alongside an ideal self with many "shoulds" and "oughts" regarding our behavior and character. The shame of being imperfect begins when we are very young, both at home and in the culture in which we worship. In situations in which our actions and our core sense of self are not separated in the scolding, we are likely to feel that we are flawed beyond repair.

In *Shame and Grace* Lewis Smedes writes about himself:

> What I felt most [in church] was a glob of unworthiness that I could not tie down to any concrete sins I was guilty of. What I needed more than pardon was a sense that God accepted me, owned me, held me, affirmed me, and would never let go of me even if he was not too much impressed with what he had on his hands.[5]

What Smedes is describing is set into the minds and hearts of very young children in Sunday school when we tell them that our purpose in life is to become perfect, as God in heaven is perfect.

Christian culture widens the gap between the real self and the ideal self (the ego and the superego) by making the ideal even more unobtainable. The more we are told to be perfect, the more we are likely to experience failure. A recent experience I had as a guest pastor will illustrate. When I arrived thirty minutes before the service, there were two cars in the back lot. I parked and went up the disability-accessible ramp to the only door I could see. It was locked. I knocked, but it did not produce anyone. I walked around the block to the street side of the building and found two more locked doors. I returned to the back of the building to find one door, invisible from my parking spot. This door was open. It had a flight of stairs up and a flight of stairs down, but no sign of a person and no sign of which way to go. I wandered upstairs and came across two people. They said "good morning" politely without approaching me. They offered me no handshake, no words of welcome. My robe was over my arm, but no one said, "Let me show you where you can hang that." I thought about the texts in the Bible about practicing hospitality. I felt as if I had managed to get in by breaking and entering! This was the emotional field that I crossed into. Was the guest preacher perceived as a threatening outsider?

There were other signs that this was a shame-bound congregation. As I walked in and out of the sanctuary, I overheard several conversations. A man and a woman were talking about the placement of the pews. I said "good morning," and again I was not offered a word of welcome. One of them smiled; the other gave me a look that said, "We're in a conversation here; don't interrupt." Taking this clue, I said with a lighthearted tone, "If you are talking about moving the pews, you must be people of great courage." The woman scowled.

When she walked into the pastor's office a few minutes later, I discovered that she was to be the lay reader. Her first comment was, "The last time we had a guest preacher she sat over by the pulpit the whole time, instead of up behind the altar where the pastor is *supposed* to sit." I was getting the blame for someone else's imperfection! My hope of avoiding failure was significantly lowered. All of my experiences of being shamed by other congregations for not living up to some perfection they had hoped for flooded my emotional memory. It only took being locked out, ignored, and wrongfully shamed to convince me of the dangers of the present assignment. But dogged in my pursuit of redemption, I asked for very specific instructions on where to sit.

She informed me that I would walk down the aisle on her left and sit on her left in the chancel area. By her tone of voice it was clear to me that she believed that I would mess it up no matter what I did. But the service proceeded, and I gave it my best.

Her first words after the service were these: "Well (sigh) . . . I guess that since we say the Lord's Prayer every Sunday we won't miss having left it out today." Again, my imperfection was pointed out to me. You know you are in a shame culture when blame is the order of the day. It never occurred to her that she had some responsibility for the inclusion of the Lord's Prayer in the service. She had been sitting there the entire time, so why didn't she stand up and add it in when I missed it? The blame was ingrained and insidious.

Here's how that experience looks from the perspective of the church as a shame culture. A certain level of perfection was required, even of new visitors! If you manage to find your way in, you better know your place, follow directions, and keep quiet about what you see and especially about what you feel. You'll probably be blamed for something someone else did, and you'll learn that the rules are more important than whatever you have to offer. You won't be told all of the rules, but you will be criticized for failing to obey them. You won't be welcomed with open arms; in fact, you'll be seen as a potential threat to the system by bringing in outside ideas and agendas. You'll embarrass us if you say anything about our imperfection. You'll learn not to laugh about anything, because we can't laugh at ourselves. And if you notice that we are ashamed of ourselves, we will feel even more ashamed.

I left the service in a fog of despair. I had agreed to preach two Sundays in this church while the pastor was gone. Luckily, the second Sunday was a totally different experience, which I will talk about later. For now, it stands as a perfect illustration of one woman's ability, supported by the culture around her, to shame one person for her imperfection.

Self-denial

> "If any want to become my followers, let them deny themselves . . . and follow me." (Mark 8:34)

The denial of pleasure is a key element in the religious shaming of our sexual desires and passions. The Christian culture has long advocated the denial and fear of pleasure. The flip side of this attitude is that those who engage in pleasurable sexual activity do so with an accompanying dose of shame.

In the counseling center where I work, many couples come to us because of their Christian backgrounds. A significant number of women come to treatment who have a delay in or absence of orgasm. In many of these cases the women have been traumatized not by prior abuse but by the ideal of Christian self-denial. To engage in healthy orgasmic activity takes a certain level of self-esteem and allowing oneself pleasure. In strict Christian cultures women are denied selfhood to the point of an inability to participate in sexual exchange as a self with feelings of pleasure. You have heard people joke about the fact that our grandmothers had sex but they didn't *enjoy* it. Sexual "dysfunction" is the inverse of the shame of the communities in which they learned to be women and to keep their rightful places.

The denial of pleasure is experienced in the culture by laughter that arises not in the pure fun of talking about sexuality but in the embarrassment one feels if the subject comes up in church. "Deny yourself and take up your cross" is a message that has been thrust at our sexuality. If you are single, deny your passion, and live and enjoy celibacy. Even within marriage there is a certain taboo against pleasure. Christian rituals do not include celebrations of sexual maturity; instead we honor first communion or confirmation. Even in our marriage services we refer to joy and faithfulness without any language that gives permission for indulgence in orgasmic pleasure.

Our culture shapes our ability to allow pleasurable sensation. When the five-year-old pastor's son stood on the front steps of the church with his dad one Sunday, he looked cute and innocent. When he asked one of the older women, "Do you have a penis?" she was horrified. His mother, quick to correct him, said, "God doesn't want us to talk about that now." The boy didn't talk about it for a long, long while. And entering into puberty wasn't easy. He internalized the thought that God wouldn't like anything about his penis, and that if talking about it was bad, doing anything with it would be criminal.

Our beliefs that God punishes those who do "naughty" things can be carried from childhood into adulthood and from the pew into the bedroom. Couples who experience difficulty achieving orgasms have internalized the judgments of the culture. One client told her therapist: "Every time we get naked, I have to say to my imaginary pastor, 'It's okay, and we don't need you in the room; go on and get out.'" For those who deny their own sexual feelings, healing takes place when they are able to rid themselves of the distorted messages of their Christian culture. Only when we believe that God wants us to have pleasure can we begin to give ourselves freely in sexual exchange. Voices of punishment from the Christian culture inhibit the free-flowing exchange of love that is so necessary in healthy sexual play.

Deny yourself sexually? Jesus allowed his head to be stroked, his feet to be oiled, and his body to be touched and drained of its power. God embodied a human being and must surely understand its passions. Engagement in healthy sexual play involves feasting yourself and your partner. We have misunderstood and misused self-denial to the point of increasing shame.

Idealism

"Go therefore and make disciples of all nations." (Matt. 28:19)

At the end of the Gospel of Matthew the church is given its mission: "Go therefore and make disciples of all nations, baptizing them in the name of the Father and of the Son and of the Holy Spirit, teaching them to observe all that I have commanded you" (Matt. 28:19-20). Every year when I go to my annual meeting, on the first day the conference statistician reads the awful news to us. Numbers of members in the conference have been declining nearly every year for the twenty years I have attended. There are exceptional growing churches, and there are new churches. But the overall number of persons becoming new disciples has been declining. We start the meeting singing "And Are We Yet Alive?" We are not so sure. We begin with a corporate experience of failure.

Evidence abounds that the church is failing in its mission to evangelize the world. The silence we share about all things sexual contributes to this decline. The numbers don't lie. Religious publishers have flooded the market with books about the ways we are failing to evangelize successfully. Marketing teams and consultants have been called in. Words like "revitalization" have worked their way into our vocabulary. There is a sense among a majority of clergy and laity alike that the institution is failing in its efforts to convince the world of the significance of Jesus Christ.

Most mainline congregations recognize this decline but have not found ways to reverse it. Herein lies the place of shame. We watch the growing influence of Eastern religions in our communities and the competition for families on Sunday mornings to play soccer rather than attend church. Buddhism and other Eastern religions are growing faster than Christianity. When those of Christian culture hear about this, they experience shame regarding their failure to achieve their core mission. Leaders double their efforts, read the best resources, take up innovative programs and worship styles, and still watch the numbers decline. The more that a congregation experiences shame in its general culture, the more shame is found in the sexual arena.

I preached one Sunday to a congregation in which all but twelve out of the eighty people in attendance were over seventy years old. I found myself wanting to throw my sermon aside and just walk out into the congregation and say, "Don't you folks realize that in fifteen years from now you won't have a church here anymore?" To do this, of course, would be to fly in the face of all taboos about congregational life. It would be rude and unkind. It would actually heap shame upon one of the sources of their decline—their shame.

This congregation had a hard time feeling good about itself. It was an urban church of middle- and upper-class white people set in a neighborhood that had become blue collar and was filling with African American and Hispanic people. Jesus' mandate to evangelize the whole world wasn't being fulfilled. What would motivate them to walk the neighborhoods for new recruits? What would help them proclaim the gospel in their own neighborhood? Could they accomplish any outreach if they felt ashamed of the realities of their decline?

When a client comes into my office feeling the weight of shame, I must be very careful not to shame them for feeling shame. Even using the word *shame* can lock them up into shame behaviors—self-denigration, silence, and hiding. I carefully use questions like, "How do you feel about yourself when you tell me this?" And I ask them to tell me about their ideals and how they measure themselves against their ideals.

To open a shame-bound culture to the truth risks punishments greater than death—the smearing of your reputation, the upheaval of the entire organization, and the breaking up of the fellowship. What if some members of the church wanted to say that they too had noticed the decline? What if some of them wanted to openly address the silence of the church in the midst of a sexual revolution, while others were in a stage of intense denial? In a shame-bound culture speaking the truth adds shame to shame.

Many congregations today are diseased and threatened with death and at the same time deeply embarrassed. This general and broader shame sets the stage for more specific sexual shame. In the next few sections I will describe aspects of church culture that lead me to consider it a shame culture.

The church's very mission is to evangelize the world, starting with the neighborhood in which it lives. On Martin Luther King Jr.'s birthday I once preached about the reality that our almost entirely white congregation was mandated by the gospel to become more inclusive. This touched a deep place of shame among the leaders and elders. They unleashed a ton of blame on me for this sermon. They wrote letters to the bishop (who was an African American man). The bishop read the sermon and exonerated me, even praised me for naming the truth. But I had underestimated the depth of the congregation's shame. The call of the gospel was once again a place of failure to them rather than a call to new life—a symptom of a shame-bound culture.

The church's shame falls in the disparity between the ideal—"Follow me, and I will make you fish for people" (Matt. 4:19)—and the reality of institutional decline. Several of the members apologized to me before worship started: "It's summertime, you know, and well, attendance really falls off," and, "When the pastor is gone, you know. . . ." I nodded my head in sympathy.

It didn't take long to make my assessment of the shame-bound nature of this congregation. The field is ripe for the harvest, and the laborers are fewer and fewer. Without a change in this particular feeling of having failed in its core mission, new members will not join. They can sometimes feel the sense of failure in the organization at a deeply unconscious level. A redefining of the goals and a clear and achievable mission statement and plan for ministry are the only relief for this overall sense of falling short.

Gender Domination

"A wife is bound as long as her husband lives." (1 Cor. 7:39)

I work with women clients who have no economic or personal power. Their husbands expect them to be servants in their homes. They labor without pay: They cook, clean, organize, look after children, and tend to their husband's needs. These women experience sexual servanthood as well. Some have tried to have control over the times and places of sexual encounters and have been raped as a result. Time and again I am told by many of them that they find sex to be uncomfortable and disgusting.

These women engage in sexual practices that feel shameful to them and yet feel the shame to be redeemable if they are pleasing their men and therefore doing what God wants. In their Christian traditions they are supposedly forgiven and made well again by doing the right thing in the order of the creation, which man and God oversee.

They do not talk to me about feeling satisfied with this arrangement or experiencing the grace of their lives being in line with God's plan for them. They tell me that God hates divorce and that their pastors have told them to go back home and do whatever the man wants them to do. They tell me about the sexual clothing that they are expected to wear, the pornography in their homes, the times when they resisted and were raped. They have little or no erotic fantasies or desires because they feel themselves to be powerless in their relationships. Many of them are deeply ashamed of their own sexuality and that of their spouses.

The idea that a woman is bound to her husband in Christian servanthood places her in a position of powerlessness, if not abuse.

We have been told in our churches that the goal is for the woman to give herself voluntarily to her husband. And no one mentions that while he is bigger and physically stronger, he has the advantage in any argument. In the wild, larger animals handicap themselves when they engage in playful contact. No one preaches to men about handicapping themselves so those women can play freely with them without fear. When we tell women to be servants voluntarily, we forget to tell the men to let go of their power, dominance, and belief in their privilege. That we have not taught families about equal, loving partnerships contributes to sexual and family violence.

A great deal of suffering is taking place because of the theologically reinforced hierarchy of God the Father, Jesus, man, and lastly women and children. For those churches that yet espouse this order of power and value, women can never live up to the ideal because the ideal is to be a man. No matter how much she does, she will yet be measured and found unworthy. The language of this oppression is embedded in worship, committee life, and programmatic ministries.

The transformation of the notion of servanthood for women is crucial to healing their shame. While power alone cannot liberate one from shame, it is an element of the healing process. Place and status are cultural constrictions that may be reduced in the grace-seeking church.

A key element in the recovery from sexual shame for a woman who is molested or raped is her need to be the one to control and start or stop any sexual encounter. By teaching her and her partner to honor any feelings of fear that arise in her during sexual foreplay and intercourse, she may again learn to trust. Without this, she will actually mentally disconnect from the experience and be only half present. She cannot love fully until she has the power to say no and to have the no respected any and all times that she says it. How can these couples learn to reshape their sexual lives until men adopt a stance of compassion (the root word of *compassion* means "suffering with") toward their female partners?

Men's shame about sex also results from the sanctification of the model of men in charge of women's lives. Reducing the worth of their partners reduces their own worth. When a woman is seen as an object, no one gains respect. Men who see their own drives for sexual pleasure as nothing more than a release of tension or the gaining of power through rape and molestation are deeply ashamed. In the complexity of male and female sexual relationships and in same-gender relationships, the church could use its voice to equalize power and to teach sexual respect. In so doing we would begin to heal this aspect of cultural shame.

Christlikeness

> "As many of you as were baptized into Christ have clothed yourselves with Christ." (Gal. 3:27)

John Berecz and Herbert Helm Jr. note a serious problem with Christian education:

> In many Sunday schools, and parochial elementary schools, children are taught to copy Jesus as the perfect pattern. How could you find a higher ideal than the incarnate God? This virtually guarantees that the person will grow up to experience lifelong shame. The prospect of eliminating the disparity between the real self and the ideal self when the ideal self is a photocopy of Jesus are dim indeed.[6]

Many of us grew up in Sunday school where the first simple lesson was "be like Jesus." The recent version of this is found in the popular bracelets and necklaces for children and teens that say WWJD (What would Jesus do?). This reminder is given to young Christians so that they can model their daily decisions after Jesus. When the decision is to share your tuna fish sandwich at lunch, the question is helpful. Of course you'd do it; Jesus broke bread and shared it with others. But what happens when the decision is more complicated, like "Would it be okay to try cigarettes?" or the emerging adolescent's question, "Is sex a good thing or a bad thing?" The question "What would Jesus do?" can be challenging to answer. The Bible says nothing about Jesus and cigarettes, and Jesus said nothing about sex.

What would a young person struggling with the decision to have sex with a boyfriend/girlfriend do? Here the idea that all of our behavior can be modeled on Jesus falls short. Was Jesus celibate? Did he have a sexual relationship with Mary of Magdala? Is there anything in the Bible suggesting that two people must be married by state law to form a "marriage" in the sight of God? If we consider any sexual behavior that is not biblical to be shameful, we set up a great deal of confusion, and we open the door wider for sexual shame.

Sunday after Sunday preachers talk to congregations about living life as Christ lived his life. This belief helps those who have tendencies to think of themselves as unworthy sinners to strive to overcome their carnality by "higher" living. The results, however, create an even larger gap between the ideal and the human reality. As Robert Albers notes: "The person with a shame-based identity reasons that one of the ways to avoid the painful experience of shame is to live perfectly or flawlessly, thus theoretically eliminating any possibility for criticism or attack which would elicit shame."[7]

The theology espoused from most pulpits could actually be attracting members who live with a great deal of inner shame. They come to the congregation looking for like-minded people who will be attempting to rid themselves of unworthiness by outward striving and acceptable beliefs and behaviors. These persons are drawn into the life of the church and often move quickly to positions of power and prestige.

In a small northern California town a new family came to church for about a month before joining. They felt at ease with the people in the congregation. They described their new worship community as a place that "felt like home." Before long they began to talk to church leaders about ways to be more involved in the life of the church. They had little to say about their last church experience except that it was "awful" and "painful." Then with cheery smiles they would say, "It'll be different here."

By the end of the year the husband and wife were both on committees, offering input and placing a good deal of time and money into remodeling a room to become the church library. They were intent on making a good outward appearance. The pastor sensed that they had some inner shame or some personal secret that they kept deeply hidden. When a church debate broke out, they became the worst of the gossips in the community and the first to condemn both the pastor and leaders as "unchristian." These people were out looking for the ideal church and couldn't tolerate that this one too had a few flaws. They were looking for a place where everyone was just like Jesus, and they couldn't tolerate that this one had ordinary people in it. They were trying to rid themselves of their own negative feelings and low esteem by joining a place where everyone was Christlike. When perfect Christlikeness is the goal, the ordinary preacher and the ordinary believer can never feel that he or she measures up.

In the area of sex we cannot turn to Jesus as a model. We can look to his loving and healing actions, but we do not have a clue whether he engaged in sexual intercourse. This reality may, in fact, largely contribute to the repression of all things sexual in Christendom for centuries.

Congregations shame their members by expecting them to be perfectly Christlike. A woman told me recently that she wasn't going back to her church because she had "burned out." This is a familiar story. But underneath the "burned out" language were a number of other issues: lack of affirmation, lack of the experience of achieving with a team of like-minded others, and lack of genuine belief that what one does can make a difference.

The striving of congregations and church leaders for perfection is part of the burnout problem. Leaders who serve with passion are often left to feel that no matter what they contribute, "it isn't good enough." This is generally the feeling of leaders in shame-bound congregations.

Unworthiness

"I . . . beg you to lead a life worthy of the calling." (Eph. 4:1)

The Christian culture of unworthiness runs deep in our veins. On Sunday we go to worship to confess our sins, but often the language of the rituals suggests that we cannot be forgiven. We are unworthy to come to the table—unworthy, like John the Baptist, to touch Jesus' sandals.

A friend of mine called me after church on the second Sunday in Lent and said, "Why do I go to church during Lent, anyway? I went to church this morning in a pretty good mood, and by the time I walked out, I felt awful." What she experienced that morning was the pastor's confessing her own problems in an effort to find some kind of redemption in the Scripture, but even she wasn't hopeful that she could be saved, let alone anyone else.

I'm a family counselor. I spend a lot of time with people who feel unworthy of Christ's grace. Shame is that vague feeling of unworthiness, that voice in us that says, "If they really knew who I was, they'd hate me." It's the inner critic who hangs his or her head and whispers, "I'll never measure up." If we do the wrong things, if we love the wrong people, if we have sexual drives and try to meet them, we experience doubt that we will be deemed worthy when Christ returns to take everyone into glory. Early experimentation, an affair, an abortion, a same-gendered love, and a child we gave up for adoption—all are signs of our unworthiness.

Classical Christian theology teaches that we must first acknowledge that we are sinners and then take a step toward salvation. To give God glory, you have to be worthless and undeserving. The more worthless and undeserving you are, the more God can do through Christ's suffering on the cross for you. Elizabeth Clephane in 1872 penned a hymn we sing in Lent, "Beneath the Cross of Jesus," in which she asserts: "I take, O Cross, thy shadow for my abiding place . . . content to let the world go by, to know no gain nor loss, my sinful self my only shame, my glory all the cross."[8] This has been the traditional Christian theologian's view of human unworthiness, that it is a prerequisite to Christ's glory.

I don't believe that this is truly biblical theology. I believe that theologians have attempted to make Christ look even more holy than he is by knocking us down a peg. This is the dynamic in a male-female abusive relationship. The dominant male must have a submissive partner who is only tied to him by his benevolent good will. Without him she would be nothing. Have we co-opted this understanding of an abusive relationship and given it to God and the church? Or have abusers learned it in church?

Our unworthiness and total debasement have been seen as the proof of God's great love for us. It would take a human sacrifice of enormous glory to rid us of our imperfection. Christ will erase our shame at the moment of the resurrection. The problem with this atonement theory is that once people feel themselves unworthy, change is a slow and difficult process. Once someone is convinced that he or she has deep character flaws, that person will struggle for a long while before accepting the power of the resurrection. In the church calendar Easter is a much longer season than Lent, but we say less about people's worth and value during that time than we say about their sinful, awful selves the seven weeks of Lent. Our very theology of the atonement as the place where Christ is sacrificed suggests that we too must be sacrificed (crucified) before we can be resurrected. This is a dangerous theology.[9]

We need to view the cross from the perspective of Christ's resistance rather than his sacrifice. His resistance to the powers of death made it possible for him to take the consequences. His commitment to truth-speaking, healing, and loving actions resulted in his ultimate death and his glory. The cross may be seen as the place of liberation from shame and the resurrection as a power that we too may share, as we seek to love one another, liberating us from sin and unworthiness. Jesus did not go to the cross ashamed. He did not die there in unworthiness. There is no honor in self-degradation. There is honor in following through on your conviction to love. This is the first step toward salvation.

While churches are not likely to do away with Lent, we can be clear about the messages that we preach. If our people are too shame-bound in Lent, they will miss the good news of the liberation of their lives in Easter.

Condemnation

> "... The wicked will not stand in the judgment, nor sinners in the congregation of the righteous." (Ps. 1:4)

Who enforces the rules in a shame-bound culture? In Christianity it is none other than God "Himself." Lewis Smedes notes:

> A snoop is one thing. A watchful parent is another. Is God like those hidden television cameras that stare day and night into every jail cell or scan every nook of the department store where we shop? ... What can we do with this God who sees all and knows all?[10]

Some children are taught with a shame statement, such as "God will punish you for that," and they spend the rest of their lives trying to avoid God's wrath. Facing death, many lifelong Christians still doubt the possibility that they will get into heaven. The fear of God's eternal damnation reflects their inner shame.

A woman was in the hospital and asked for a visit with the chaplain. Marie went to have a chat with her. The woman was near the end of her life, and she was reviewing everything. She told Marie, "Some while ago I converted to Catholicism in order to worship at my daughter's church. I don't feel much like a Catholic. I was raised Lutheran. In my heart I still feel like a Lutheran." She paused and tears flooded her eyes. "Do you think that God will punish me for faking it like that—pretending to be Catholic and taking communion with my daughter?" "Does God have a particular denomination?" Marie asked her, smiling. "No, I suppose not."

Frequently people nearing death review their moral behavior. When my father's uncle asked the pastor at the graveside, "Will he make it into heaven?" I boiled with rage. The idea that my uncle had the job of determining his own brother's fitness for heaven had come from his faith community. He was part of a culture of shame. In his church dancing and card playing were sins. Sex between a husband and wife was tolerable but not to be mentioned. And sex for others, including my gay father, was an "abomination." Many people feel that a regretted sexual behavior will seal their fate when it comes to the afterlife. They have been taught this by a culture of sexual shame.

A friend of mine has a fascination for stone-carved angels that adorn grave monuments. On a tour of a local graveyard she led me to a mausoleum at the top of a hill overlooking our valley. It stood nearly six feet tall, and except for fading in the lettering, it had withstood nearly 150 years without damage. On the side toward town and the rest of the graveyard was the epitaph of the town pastor "Reverend William Wesley Smith" with a tribute in quotations and italics that read, "Well done, good and faithful servant." On the other side, toward bracken and an overgrowth of trees was the name of the pastor's wife, "Rebecca Anne Smith." Rebecca's epitaph was in ornate script and quite small. I might have missed the wording had my friend not stopped and pointed it out to me. It read simply, "She did what she could."

Rebecca died a victim of the shame of her Christian culture. She wasn't perfect. Perhaps she allowed herself the pleasures of life, perhaps she failed to convert all of her friends, perhaps she never fully became Christlike in her lifetime, perhaps she died in fear of a judging God and just hoped for the best. After all, "She did what she could" is a tribute to an ordinary human being. I want it proudly placed on my own grave as a sign that I have resisted the shame in which I was taught the commandments and precepts of the Christian faith.

Questions for Reflection

1. What labeling goes on around you in your congregation, family, and work?
2. Make a list of the names and labels you hear at church.
3. Discuss "perfection" as a goal for Christian living.
4. Does your church expect the pastor to be perfect? If so, how? If not, why not?
5. Does your faith community suffer from a sense of failure or unworthiness?
6. The author suggests that women need to engage in sexual exchanges that give them equal power with their partners. Do you agree or disagree, and why?
7. In *Release for Trapped Christians*[11] Flora Wuellner suggests that rather than imitating Christ, people can aim to "abide" in Christ. Are "imitating" and "abiding" different?
8. How does your congregation send out the message that you might never "measure up"?
9. Does a sexual sin hold greater consequence than other sins?
10. Do you think there will be sex in heaven?

13. Methods of Healing

This book has attempted to lead the reader through the healing process for sexual shame. In the first chapters we looked at possible diagnoses of the problem. Subsequent chapters examined the urgent need for solutions, including some discomforting material. Now we turn our thoughts to models for healing. By now the reader is fully aware of the painful effects of the underlying sexual shame in the body of Christ. Grave concerns have been raised that the Christian church perpetuates shame. The first step in congregational healing is to confront the silence and the denial with an experience of "tough love."

Speaking the Truth

An element of confrontation is often the first step in the healing process. Parents use "tough love" to put boundaries on acting-out teenagers. Members of the alcoholic's family get together to confront the drinker about the extent of his or her problem. Those who see the problem and its effects are best able to help the person in denial. Armed with lists of the ways the addict's behavior creates pain for them, family members lovingly cut through the pretense. In this style of confrontation people are helped to see that the problems are painfully real.

With the exception of the most traumatized or most seriously mentally ill, the confrontation process can be used as a step toward healing. When someone laden with sexual shame needs healing, the first step is that he or she acknowledge the full weight of remorse. This is tricky in work with victims because they may already feel responsible and burdened with more than their fair share of the regrets. Victims need to talk about their shame and to be heard with compassion.

With perpetrators of sexual shame denial is a very strong protective shield that only firm and loving challenge can penetrate. Those who have shamed others need to experience the pain that was lying under their act of violation, and the pain the shamed one experienced. I believe that most individuals and most congregations are healthy enough to experience corporate remorse. What I am suggesting here, then, is a safe and loving but also confrontational process that heals sexual shame.

At a nearby hospital the staff decided to hold a brief service of prayer on Sunday afternoons. The announcement on the overhead speaker said, "A brief interfaith service will be held at eleven a.m. in the chapel on the third floor." The nursing supervisor heard the announcement and was puzzled. What she heard was that the chaplain was having a brief "in your face" service. What we hear is often what we expect at an unconscious level, and this always grows out of our experience. The supervisor had grown up in a church in which she felt that the sermons were always "in your face."

How do we heal the church without a confrontation with those who engage in shaming behaviors? On a large scale it has never worked well to place blame on whole groups or categories of people or behavior. Group blame led to the crusades, the witch trials, the Holocaust, and ethnic and religious cleansing. It has not been effective in limiting the influence or power of those who deal with their own shame by tossing it onto others. So we have only begun to notice the amount of work that needs to be done to heal sexual shame.

Learning to Assess a Congregation

The healing process begins with an honest and thorough assessment of the problems. A local church could do its own research to determine the level of shame within it. Perhaps a research team could be put together to devise a quick survey about shame. Do people get messages in church that they should be ashamed of themselves? How often and in what ways? Do people have experiences of feeling shunned or picked on for their beliefs, actions, or words? Rate your church on a scale of one to ten, with "one" meaning that no one feels ashamed or blames or shames anyone else, and "ten" meaning that almost everyone is shaming or feeling ashamed. What is the shame level in your congregation around sexual thoughts, activities, or orientations?

How would people who have left your congregation rate your shame level? As a leader or participant in your congregation, how would you rate your own shame level? Use these quick surveys as a starting point for your assessment. Then go deeper. What secrets has the congregation kept over the years? What sexual secrets have been gossiped about? How have "illegitimate" pregnancies been spoken of? How many members of the congregation are living together? Are they spoken of as "living in sin"?

Preaching "from house to house" as I do, I have had the opportunity to assess the level of shame emanating from the pulpit, the fellowship, and the language of the liturgy. For my own protection, as a child raised with shame and secrets, I find that I need a congregation that is light with grace and understands the difference between behavior and worth. I also seek out congregations in which laughter is frequent and we all know that mess-ups are just a part of life. I look for places where experimentation is okay and where people's sexual attractions, gender, and sexual practices do not exclude them from the circle of God's love. I look for places where equality and justice and liberation get a lot of airtime. These are congregations without shame.

What it all boils down to is that some congregations are too steeped in shame to be mended in our lifetimes. They will die their own painful deaths. Meanwhile the Scriptures call us to seek life. Here is a list of things to look for.

Symptoms of Shame-Bound Congregations
- New visitors and "outsiders" are perceived as threatening to the church.
- Communication is focused on mistakes and problems (blame) rather than strengths and possibilities.
- Discussion stays focused on surface issues; underlying affective experience is discounted.
- Leaders are anxious in the face of change.
- The congregation is overly apologetic about its own failures (shame begets shame).
- Conflicts remain the same for years without resolution.
- New members experience a disparity between what is shown on the outside on Sunday morning and the "real" work of the church in committees.
- Issues are couched in "right or wrong" terms.
- There is little or no humor.
- A lot of attention is focused on a few people who control the church's agenda.
- People don't talk openly or directly about shameful, abusive, or compulsive behavior.
- The congregation denies the effects of the symptoms listed above.

- Dress and behavior codes are strictly adhered to.
- Congregational energy is used up with infighting, and there is a perception that there are not enough resources for missions.

Contrasting Virtues of Shame-Free Congregations
- New visitors and "outsiders" are given places of honor.
- Communication is full of affirmation, naming strengths and possibilities.
- Discussion deepens intimacy and focuses on feelings and faith.
- Leaders welcome change.
- Wounds are acknowledged, confession offered, worthiness restored.
- Conflicts are resolved with mutual satisfaction.
- The working community and the worshiping community are the same.
- Issues are couched in "win-win" terms.
- Humor abounds.
- People empower each other.
- Shaming, abusive, or compulsive behavior is named and stopped.
- Space is made for people to raise any subject of joy or concern.
- Dress and behavior is flexible, individual, and spontaneous.
- Congregations minimize administrative bickering and details, while maximizing mission, outreach programs, and resources.

Recovery
Once an area of shame or a person who has the tendency to shame others is identified, the process of healing can be devised. The model used for addiction recovery could be a resource. While I have not said that the church is addicted to shame, I have said that some elements of the addictive cycle, including denial, silence, secrets, and defensiveness, exist in many congregations. These elements may be healed in a model borrowed from addiction recovery programs. In addition, the style of healing in the addiction community involves confrontation that is well thought out and is rooted in the intention of healing love. It is designed to heal both the perpetrator who is ashamed and the victim who is shamed. Remember, too, that the perpetrators are likely victims of someone else's sexual shame.

While we explore possible solutions to the church's longstanding participation in the infliction of shame, we must be careful not to enter a shame-for-shame game that leaves everyone more wounded than before. Nevertheless, a significant step in the healing of shame that the church may borrow includes a rather "in your face" conversation between the wounded ones and the perpetrators. Confrontational healing for those who have acted out their sexual shame on others actually involves forcing the perpetrators to acknowledge their wrongdoing and to feel their shame.

The police arrested the church custodian (let's call him "Al") a few days after a report had been filed by the parent of one of the teenagers at the church. One night after youth group, he had walked the girl to her car and had chatted with her until long after the others had gone home. Alone with her, his demeanor changed, and he assaulted and sexually molested her.

Unknown to any of the church parents or staff, this was not Al's first arrest. He had been the church janitor for less than a year, and the church had not asked for a police record, fingerprints, or other details about him when they hired him. His references had appeared to be sound.

Al was, by the definition of the parole officer, a repeat sex offender. He was put into a group process at the county jail with other men who had the same problem. The group process allows men like Al to discuss their abuse, which is very painful. Most of the men are not only perpetrators but also sexual abuse victims. Men like Al find it hard to talk about their actions. They are ashamed of their past, afraid of their feelings, and closely guarded. The staff became aware, by the psychologist's report, that Al was severely traumatized in childhood. If he were to cut through his machismo to that pain, it would erupt with an unpredictable force. The staff also knew that Al would not be healed unless he could find and address his own shame.

In the second week of treatment Al was introduced to his shame through the stories of visitors to the program. Women victims were invited to the program and urged to describe the pain they have lived with as a result of molestation. Al was at last moved to consider the effects of his own abuse. His healing process began with the experience of *feeling* his underlying shame.

This method was effective because it took place in a very safe and controlled environment. Communication boundaries ensured that no one would be revictimized by negative comments. People were required to speak from their own experience. Their stories were in no way doubted or dismissed. They spoke about the details of the events, but more importantly, they were challenged to express the pain they had endured at that time and throughout their lifetimes. The power of their stories opened the hearts of some of the perpetrators who began to experience their own pain. The staff guided each person toward owning his or her participation in creating or experiencing pain. Elements of this process borrowed by the church today can help the healing begin.

How could the church help the young woman whom Al had victimized with her pain? By respecting her privacy, but not covering it up as if it never happened. By being adamant that her behavior, looks, or circumstances had in no way contributed to her assault. By being clear that her status as a fully beloved and respected member of the youth group and church had not changed in light of her victimization. By confessing that the hiring committee had played a part in endangering her. By offering her a public apology for that endangerment. By keeping the shame off of everyone.

In the midst of a crisis of sexual shame, the church needs to respond with a great deal of compassion. Many congregations use the expertise of people from the mental health field to facilitate healing processes. When an incident like this one occurs, the church needs to be treated like a traumatic stress victim, with great gentleness.

Is it possible or even appropriate to attempt to heal people's shame on a much larger scale? Since shame is perpetuated through our theology, misogyny, and hierarchy, healing the whole church is beyond our capability. Instead we can step back and see how it might work with one incident and one individual at a time.

Opening the church for healing might require some "in your face" services. Loving confrontations may be experienced as conflicts. When gay, lesbian, bisexual, and transgender members and their families and friends demand inclusion, it is not initially comfortable. Those who cross or blur gender boundaries awaken our own sexuality and gender issues. Women and men who seek liberation from sex-role stereotypes demand that people restructure their home lives, the ways they reach decisions, their power in the family and in the bedroom. Teens and young adults who plan to be sexually active without legal marriage ask prickly questions that confront centuries of biblical interpretation.

There is political precedent for confrontation as a route to healing. Integration in Southern churches in the late sixties and seventies included a great deal of confrontation. A superintendent recently commented that the movement for sexual justice is as powerful in his time of leadership as the racial justice movement was for those who joined the protest in that day. The church has been involved in radical justice movements for generations.

Social psychologists studying integration found an interesting phenomenon: When people thought that schools wouldn't be desegregated, they maintained their negative and prejudicial attitudes toward blacks. Once they realized that they would in fact have to be sending their children to school with black students, their opinions of blacks began to change.[1] This is a phenomenon that might predict the eventual unbiased inclusion of gay members. When congregations begin to see that integration of social minorities is inevitable, their resistance to it will greatly reduce. According to social psychologists, persons who think that change is on the horizon will begin to shift their opinions.

The confrontation of shaming behaviors and attitudes doesn't sound like what most of us go to church for. A majority of older members in local congregations want the church to comfort them as they go into their last years surrounded by the surety of their long-held, validated positions. The struggle between those who attend worship to reinforce the status quo and those who go to challenge it, however, is not a new development.

The story of Jesus overturning tables and driving out the money-changers from the temple, for example, is not included in the ecumenical lectionary of preaching texts. Scripture texts on women as victims are not highlighted on Sunday morning. We prefer the pastoral images of Jesus and forget that he himself leveled challenges to the old ways. It was precisely these challenges that led him to the cross. Jesus stands as a clear model for how to confront others without shaming them. He dealt with the demon-possessed man called "Legion" without fear or shame. He let the unclean touch him. When his disciples tried to send away the rudest and most despicable of people, Jesus opened his arms and welcomed them. If we could learn to live with the clarity of demand and the overwhelming love of Jesus, we would cure the church of its shame and its shaming.

When Jesus and his disciples rode into Jerusalem, they confronted the powers of the state and of the church. This protest parade hailed him as the new Messiah, thus challenging the status quo. The "Jesus movement" lacked structure and a title but had the power of a political movement that shaped the world for the next two thousand years.

Jesus also allowed himself to be confronted. Matthew's Gospel records the story about a Canaanite woman who shouted at Jesus to heal her daughter who was demon possessed. When Jesus refused to give the woman a crust of bread, she did not walk away ashamed. "Lord," she said, "even the dogs have the crumbs under the table to eat" (Matt. 15:21-28). The woman was not ashamed. She held her own power and demanded that Jesus treat her with greater respect. And ever so slowly the Lord realized that he had turned away from a woman who had a right to be dealt with fairly. He allowed her confrontation to call him to attention, and he was moved to grant her requests. This is an excellent example of a way that people might confront one another with love.

Could we create healthy community forums where those who have been shunned or shamed would return to the church and confront those who have hurt them? Could the context be made safe enough that healing would take the stage rather than greater pain, division, anger, and denial? There is a great need for a safe yet confrontational process.

I told a nurse at the desk of the intensive care unit at the hospital that I was working on a book about sexual shame in the church. She rolled her eyes and pushed her chart notes aside. She looked at me and said:

> I can tell you about sexual shame in the church, but only because I left it twenty-seven years ago. I was a teenager, and I went into the office to talk to the priest at his request. He began with the pretense of discussing my confirmation class, but it quickly changed into him kissing me and fondling my breasts. I got the hell out of there. Next thing I know, my mother was sending me to confession for having kicked him in the—you know where. You bet I kicked him. God only knows what might have happened if I didn't. But all my mother said was, "I don't care what happened to you, Laurie; it wasn't right to hurt the father." I never went into the confessional booth. God, what if it was him in there? And as soon as I left home, I never set foot inside the church again.

It is easy to say that this should never have happened, but it is not an isolated case. The sad reality is that many, many individuals have left behind all of the goodness and value that the church offers, and some have even left behind their faith in God, as a result of similar experiences.

This sort of injury needs to be healed with tenderness for Laurie and by challenging the church for its complicity in sexual harassment and abuse. What would it take to get Laurie back into the faith? What kind of place would open a conversation with her that would acknowledge her violation and address it? Could she be invited to participate in a group where clergy who are sexual offenders listen to the stories of those who have been victims of clergy sexual abuse? Would she be motivated to confront and heal them and thereby also heal herself?

Perhaps I might go back to Laurie and ask her what it would take (if anything could change) to reconnect her to a worshiping community. Remember that when Matthew Fox welcomed people back to talk about the injuries they had sustained in church, he was overwhelmed by hundreds who accepted his invitation. People may be more eager than we think to be healed and to reconnect 'with loving communities.

Church-growth experts have long been telling us that it's easier to recruit new people than to go after wounded ones. Of course it is! But the wounds keep traveling down through the generations, and the grace of God and the power of congregational participation get lost along the way. I'd rather we get a little more in some people's faces and restore the church! To that end, I have written my own list of "wild ideas" for healing.

A List of Wild Ideas

Here's my list of suggestions for healing some of the sexual shame in our churches. The seeds of healing are here. Although I call them my "wild ideas," I hope that you will entertain them in earnest.

- Those who have been wounded by the church (local or otherwise) would come and tell their stories with two or three witnesses. Prayers would be offered. The listeners would offer the wounded ones apologies. They would say things like, "You don't need to be ashamed anymore," and "We are proud of you for telling the truth; we welcome you into God's grace."
- Conferences would pay for group therapy for those who have been brought up on charges of sexual misconduct and provide in-house treatment and follow-up counseling. Group process and strict accountability would be a must.
- All conferences and regions would have pastoral counselors on staff.
- Recognizing the pervasiveness of themes of shame in theology, theologians would invest themselves in biblical interpretation that redefine the related themes of suffering, sacrifice, and grace.
- Human sexuality curricula would be mandatory in seminary training. This training would include attitudes about sex and gender throughout the history of Christendom.

- Sexual education for clergy would include personal reflection about their own sexual practices as they relate to spiritual values and biblical beliefs.
- Seminary education for clergy would include practical teaching on the application of sexual education in churches today.
- Curriculum writers for denominations would more frequently include sexuality education for all grade levels.
- Workshops would be provided by conferences, regions, and judicatories on the topics of sexuality and sexual shame.
- A national interfaith center would be developed for individuals, families, and congregations dealing with Christian faith and sexual orientation issues.
- Heterosexual couples would refuse to enter legal marriage contracts until everyone—including same-sex couples—had the legal benefits of marriage. Clergy could offer only holy unions in the church for persons of all sexual orientations that would be different from legal and state-required marriage contracts. Churches would get out of the state-sanctioned business of legal marriage and focus on biblical covenants.

Questions for Reflection

1. Can you recall a time when you had to "tough love" someone in your family or in your church?
2. Identify the people in your faith community who bring light-heartedness and respect for all people into your organization.
3. Have you ever visited a congregation that felt "depressed" or "ashamed of itself"? Describe that congregation and the feelings you had while you were there.
4. Suppose you had been on the personnel committee that hired Al. What would you have felt and done after the molestation?
5. Compare and contrast the sexual justice movement with the racial justice movement.
6. Using the lists of characteristics of shame-bound congregations and shame-free congregations, check off items that relate to your congregation.
7. What did Jesus learn about shame from the Canaanite woman?
8. Read the list of wild ideas together, and discuss them.

14. Ground Rules for Conversations

Those wounded by shame are reluctant to come back into the church family. Many of the wounded have tried to talk about the issues, only to be shamed again for bringing their stories forward. Therefore the creation of space for such conversations takes a skilled facilitator, therapist, or mediation counselor. Fortunately, people with these skills are available through counseling centers across the country.

I have pointed out that the opposite of shame is respect. When a person experiences that his or her values, norms, choices, and sexuality are respected, he or she experiences acceptance. In each of us there is a deep longing for this acceptance, which is not based on how good we are, how perfectly we do our Christian duties, or how many good works we can show. We long to be accepted as we are and respected for shaping our lives as we have chosen to shape them.

When I teach listening skills to others, I must first help them keep their own judgments out of the conversation. In the church, where we allow a good deal of judgment in the name of chastisement or perfecting one another for Christ, danger lurks. So in order to have a discussion of ground rules for conversations about sexuality and shame, it is helpful to consider the role of participants' attitudes in the conversation. On the next page is a comparison of the characteristics of respectful conversations with those of shaming conversations, adapted from Merle Fossum and Marilyn Mason's work on shame in family systems.[1]

With respectful attitudes and prayerful hearts, we can open up conversations that heal shame. Whether the conversation takes place between two individuals or in small groups, the respect we offer is crucial in preventing a re-shaming experience. When a person feels worthless and devalued, our task is to build that person's esteem by respect and valuation. We enter the process remembering to put down any stones that we may have gathered to throw, and we notice not our own sins or another's but that through Christ we are forgiven of all our sins.

Respectful Conversations	Shame-Bound Conversations
Violations lead to guilt, repentance, and grace.	Violation of values leads to unpardonable shame.
Self is both separate and part of larger system.	Self has blurred boundaries.
Rules require accountability.	Rules require obedience.
Desires are discussed, and mutual agreements occur through dialogue.	Relationship is always in jeopardy so discussion is limited.
Individuals are accountable and able to negotiate compromises.	Individuals express blame and develop rigid defenses.
Values can be reappraised in light of new experiences and exegesis.	Rules and biblical values are not negotiable.
Individuals have the ability to empathize.	Alienation and distance are the norm.
Diversity is honored.	Diversity is threatening.
Individuals grow and mature into wholeness.	Individuals present false selves and resist change.
Sexuality is healthy, pleasurable, and sacramental.	Sexuality is sin, taboo, and threat.

A plan for conversations follows.

1. Select a facilitator.

The first task of a congregation is to pick a skilled person who is perceived by all the participants as fair, impartial, and compassionate. In therapy we say that if the client is not "aligned" with the therapist, no growth or healing will happen. Choosing a facilitator is a complex process that boils down to the rapport that is established. Will the congregation trust the facilitator? Does the facilitator come without bias? Is this person capable of building trust with diverse individuals in a short period of time? Is this person healed of his or her own sexual-shame issues? Finding the right facilitator for the conversation about shame will set the stage for healing.

2. Encourage the use of "I" statements.

When people who are wounded come together, they often start from a place of blame. I have described the way that shamed individuals are especially prone to seek relief from shame by placing blame elsewhere. To reduce the blaming tendencies of participants, each person is asked to speak only from his or her own experience.

People are also likely to dodge their own experience by trying to focus the conversation on opinion or theological issues. Scripture texts would most likely be used to justify a position rather than to illustrate an experience. Again, a skilled facilitator will need to keep each participant focused on his or her own experience.

In a forum that provides safety for participants, individuals can share stories from their hearts and listen to others' experiences of sexual shame. Rules and policies have no place in beginning discussions. In healthy families rules follow the process of understanding, and they are flexible and can be renegotiated in light of human concerns.

3. Invite confidentiality.

Confidentiality is the most crucial rule if people are brought together to talk about sexual shame. This ground rule may be difficult in a church in which community boundaries are regularly blurred in the name of love. For example, the prayer chain is often the center of gossip rather than a protected space for the lifting up of concerns. If pastoral-relations committees, personnel committees, or hiring committees have not maintained confidentiality about information they handle, the church may not be ready to talk more openly about sexual shame. The intense privacy of these issues requires that the church first address its tendency to spread information around the congregation and community. A safe church for discussions such as these is a church that respects personal sharing and honors the rights of individuals to tell their own stories when and if they choose to do so. Shame occurs with the turning of a personal story into a public scandal. Great care needs to be taken so that people understand the way that retelling anyone else's story violates integrity and may revictimize the other person. While no binding legal contracts can be made to protect the information shared in church groups, the leader's firm emphasis on respect and privacy is crucial.

4. Allow time to tell and hear the stories.

In the midst of a church conversation about holy unions, one man who rarely spoke up in meetings rose to his feet. "Last year," he said, "my sister and I went to L.A. to bury our brother. We had not seen him for years. He had dropped out of sight and out of the family when he announced that he was gay. It was awkward and uncomfortable to drop back into his life to sort out his belongings. What we found surprised us. On his dresser he had a worn copy of our grandmother's Bible. He had written all over it. He had a rosary by his bed and a picture of Jesus in his wallet." He paused to push back a great swell of emotion. "In all those years, I knew that my brother was gay, but I never considered that he could also be a Christian. I felt a weight of shame that's still very hard to bear. I had played a part in losing touch with him, and I hadn't even seen that we were *one* in faith. It changed me a lot."

Stories like this open people's hearts to compassion. The telling of the personal story is crucial. Some people, however, may try to tell someone else's story. The latter can be carefully discouraged. You have probably been in a meeting where someone said, "And I know a lot of other people feel this way too." This kind of comment is an attempt to bolster one's own point of view. It's a move for power. No one will be conducting an opinion poll to determine what "a lot of other people" actually think in the midst of a conversation about sexual shame. Therefore the participants are encouraged to use personal stories only.

A retired pastor in our community was active in teaching about Christianity and homosexuality. He hosted a conversation on the subject as a Sunday morning class. Twenty people came to the class. Some of them spoke for the first time about a gay, lesbian, or bisexual member of their families. One man was divorcing his wife who had disclosed that she was a lesbian. He shared his anger and his pain very honestly.

The pastor-teacher invited a prominent biblical scholar who came from the seminary to talk about the Bible. That morning ten additional visitors joined the class. They were angry about the course and adamant about their positions on the issue, and they weren't convinced of anything by the resident scholar. The tragedy of this last class was that these people would not have dared to bring so much anger to the group if they had heard the humanizing stories of the weeks before.

Discussions must be grounded in personal experience. We learned the hard way that you need to have a group "closed" when discussing sexuality. From start to finish people need to be committed to a process of learning together. Everyone suffered from not hearing others' personal reasons for having different conclusions about the biblical texts and the issue of homosexuality.

5. Provide the option to speak or to be silent.

There is a Quaker tradition wherein one person at a meeting is designated to be the observer of group process. The observer's job is to notice when and where God is active in the group. This is a wonderful model for any group discussion about something as serious as sexual shame. The Quaker meeting model is also very respectful of participants' rights to speak or to be silent as the spirit leads them.

With a topic as explosive as sexual shame, the facilitator will need to let people know that everyone wanting a turn to speak will have one and that those who wish to remain silent will be respected. If anyone feels that he or she must leave the room, the person is asked to speak with the facilitator by phone later that same day. This prevents anyone leaving the conversation in overwhelming pain and lingering isolation.

6. Encourage humor.

When it comes to sex, we are all a bit jittery. A good dose of humor may be required to have conversations about it. The facilitator's humor is essential to the healing process. Humor is the icebreaker that allows us to laugh at ourselves and to notice our humanity. Allowing or inserting humor in the conversation gives permission for people to experience a full range of emotions. When the conversation becomes loaded with either anger or sadness, the situation is ripe for shame. A stretch break may be required at any time. Encourage and include play in your time together. I remember once being told that if I needed to take care of myself in a tense meeting, I could always excuse myself and go to the bathroom. No one would ever ask!

7. Allow the expression of anger.

In individual therapy, victims heal by getting in touch with their anger. The therapist knows this and allows anger to emerge. A huge roadblock to healing in the church is that many of us long ago concluded that anger is incompatible with Christian faith. The time has come in preaching and teaching to reeducate Christians about the purpose of anger and its function for healing. A facilitated conversation allows for honest anger, stated with feeling and without blame, and can move a wounded person back to a place of power. Anger is the energy behind confrontation and it serves to boost self-esteem. For those who have been victimized, their worthiness is in doubt. Anger is the energy of self-worth.

8. Provide grace-full worship.

Song, poetry, dances, and prayer are elements of worship that ground people's conversations in God. We have unity in one healer and lover who will never misuse us or fail us in any way.

Conversations that heal have hope embedded in them: hope in the faithfulness of God and hope in the healing of the church.

I returned the second week to preach in the church in which I had been shamed by the lay leader. I went in fear and trepidation. On the steps that led to the entrance of the building was a delightful seventy-something man with a warm smile. "You must be the one," he said. "I'm glad to meet you." He walked up the stairs with me; he asked me about my work and studies. He offered to hang up my robe. He talked about his own life in teaching. When he showed me the worship area, he said that I could use the pulpit or the music stand, whichever felt best to me!

The worship that morning had a new feel to it. The entire service was printed in the bulletin, making it easy for a new person to follow along. The music at the early service had easy lyrics and guitar and oboe accompaniment. At announcement time the lay leader made a few jokes, and everyone laughed. In announcing the blood pressure clinic that morning in the pastor's office, he also said, "Well, it's a good thing that we didn't take this two weeks ago, after that big blow up in the worship committee meeting." This acknowledgment of conflict is in direct contrast to the shame-bound family rule of keeping silent about differences.

In the second service the lay leader was a young mother in her twenties. She was busy settling her two children in wheelchairs into their places. As we started I said, "Please feel free to cover me on anything I might do wrong." "Okay," she said, "but Pastor Rick messes something up every week and he's been doing this stuff for years! We love him just the same." She laughed. When I left something out of the service, she reinserted it. Afterward she was warm and appreciative. And so was I!

The experience of this second week was surprisingly different. One or two people set the stage for me, offered me welcome and grace, and thanked me for coming. The different experience I had on those two Sundays speaks to the transforming power of healed and open leaders. While the first week I had been shamed, the second week I was welcomed. The majority of the congregation would not have noticed the difference. But a newcomer certainly would. At that church, as at others, healing and growth lie in the hands of joyful, welcoming lay leaders.

9. Plan to make necessary referrals.

When people who have experienced shame through their participation in the church are invited back to talk about it, the potential for healing is high. The possibility also exists, however, that someone needing therapeutic help will use the church as a way to scapegoat his or her own issues of healing. For this reason, a skilled facilitator may need to recommend personal therapy. When an incest survivor eventually speaks the truth to her family as part of the healing, the stakes are very high. Will the family refuse to believe it? Will the family make the problem out to be the victim's fault? Will the confrontation become rage-filled? Similarly, church members who return to speak the truth to their congregations risk great harm to themselves. They need to be fully prepared for any response.

Many people who are very involved in the life of a church are seeking a better family than the one they had as children. If the church allows itself to become the person's good family rather than the recycled bad family, healing will take place.

As I discussed healing in the church with a colleague, he suggested that people who feel intense levels of shame are drawn to the shame-based nature of the church. "It's like going to the bar on Sunday morning for an alcoholic," he said. "Why do you suppose anyone does that?" "Well," I said, "what if they are actually looking for an AA group, where people like themselves have learned to lay it aside and recover from it?" He smiled.

The congregation can be the place where the shame-bound come and reverse their shame-based identity. Working with a woman who has been sober after ten years of drug and alcohol recovery work, I discovered that her fear of finding work and going back to school was that she wouldn't fit out there in the "real" world with "straight" people who aren't addicts. Although she had recovered from alcoholism and addiction, she hadn't stopped thinking of herself as an addict. People who have stopped shaming themselves or stopped feeling ashamed for someone else's sexual abuse, orientation, or behavior also need to let go of their shame-based identity.

A church that lives with a shame-based attitude or identity is not the place to find healing. The congregation that has noticed its shame and dealt with the shaming behaviors and attitudes it has perpetuated is a place of healing for people who have been ashamed or shamed. In every situation the potential is present to mend old wounds. Using the above guidelines, a facilitated process can move a congregation and individuals within and beyond it out of shame.

10. Affirm, affirm, and affirm.

When people show up to work on issues like sexual shame, they have a lot of courage. Even if they come with angry feelings, vindictive thoughts, and plans to dissect the facilitator (just joking), they need to hear that they too are respected and affirmed. If you have had conversations that are conflicted, you are likely making progress. The only people who can't be healed are the ones who aren't in the room. When people find that they can be their true selves without shame, the more they will disclose their deeper shames. The more they can be loved for their mistakes, the more they will experience forgiveness toward themselves and others.

I worked for a year with an excellent group facilitator in a congregation that was shame-bound. They had assessed it, admitted it, and decided to change it. Every month all people in leadership positions were required to come to a three-hour meeting. We played games, took on common tasks, and agreed to ground rules. We discussed the norms and values of the congregation and then the beliefs of the congregation. We conducted surveys of the congregation and of the neighborhood we served. We built up a respectful, grace-filled leadership team.

Each meeting was playful and hard work at the same time. And every meeting had an agenda item on it that took up one-third of our time. One-third of our meeting we patted ourselves on the back. Healthy pride is the opposite of shame. We praised one another and highlighted all the great things that God had been doing in and through us since we last met. We passed very specific kudos to each other and thereby raised everyone's esteem and the group's esteem. In many settings people get all the shame, and God gets all the glory. In this setting both God and the people were praised! This contagious process did more to relieve shame than any individual intervention. So, whatever else you do or don't do, affirm, affirm, affirm.

Questions for Reflection

1. With one other person, using "I" statements, talk about a time when you felt wrongfully accused.
2. Discuss ways to protect privacy and/or reduce gossip in your faith community.
3. Where does humor happen in the life of your congregation?
4. The author suggests that anger is a step in the healing process. Isn't anger a sin?
5. Do you think the church is like an AA group for the ashamed?
6. List ways that your congregation can boost its self-esteem.

15. Lifting the Shame

Building Self-Esteem in Congregations

I believe the church is still a powerful influence in the healing process for sexual shame. With core teachings on the way that God loves us, the existential value of each person is affirmed. Because our spirituality, our connection to God, can be an unfailing source of great depth of intimacy, we have to honor the power of the messages we give and receive in the religious community.

In the past twenty years we have seen a shift in the focus of ministry from the nurturing of spiritual growth and evangelism to the building up of congregations themselves. To boost sagging attendance churches have developed better marketing plans, services aimed at younger members, new children's programs, and outreach strategies. As a family therapist I experience these changes as attempted solutions to a problem that is much deeper. In fact, I am convinced that no amount of great programming will substitute for a community that appears to be unwilling to consider issues of human sexuality.

Consider your own life. Do you think you could live a healthy life without thinking about your sexuality? How can congregations have healthy lives without thinking about their positions, assumptions, denials, and affirmations of sexuality?

When psychologist Morris Rosenberg put together a research project to study the self-esteem of adolescents in New York City schools, he found a few things he wasn't expecting. For example, he found that even though their peers stigmatized African American students, African American students did not exhibit low levels of self-esteem. Their self-esteem was based more on their experience at home than it was in the cultural prejudice they daily encountered. When their parents and other adult role models had good self-esteem, the young people felt themselves to be in the midst of a great culture. Their self-esteem remained intact despite the cultural slurs and stereotypes they experienced around them.[1]

The implication of this research, for our purposes, reveals two things. First, it reveals that shame may be forced on people from the outside, but it need not penetrate the inner core of the personality. Second, it reveals that parents and siblings have the greatest influence on self-esteem. In the church family too, people long to experience positive self-esteem, and the more closely knit the community of believers is, the more powerful its influence.

Lewis Smedes' book *Shame and Grace* describes the healing process of grace. He sees "grace as God's acceptance of our whole menagerie of self."[2] While forgiveness frees us from guilt, only grace frees us from shame. With grace we experience our worthiness restored.

At a workshop on family violence it was said that the victims are the ones who teach us about the healing path. If we as a church do nothing more than dialogue with the victims of our corporate shaming, we will have come a long way. If we can earn the trust that our foreparents in the faith allowed to erode in these individuals, then we will be honored to learn the path of healing.

As a family counselor I see sexual shame overcome in very grace-filled ways. I watched a woman emerge like Rip Van Winkle from a marriage with a drunken, passed-out spouse. Her parents slashed her tires when they found out that she had gone out to coffee with a man she had met in a college class; they wanted her to stay home with her drunken husband because "that's where you belong." When I asked her how she knew she could get out of this, she said, "Oh, I don't know. Somehow God just told me I could be different from the rest of my family."

A young woman told me of four generations of incest in her family. She said that her cousin who molested his younger sister is now the youth leader at his church. I kept my clinical composure. Add it to the list, I thought. But in reality I'm angry about it, and I'm tired of holding it all in. So I wrote it down. And here I am in the section of the book where I am to give the reader the magic key that will unlock the shame-bound church, and all I have are clues.

A therapist friend of mine said, "One of the things we don't know is that we aren't stuck." The shame-bound person or congregation feels stuck. The theology that has blamed women and over-sexualized them for five thousand years isn't likely to change in several lifetimes. The theology that projected power and potency into male sexuality will not change quickly. It takes years and years to reshape people's belief systems. The lava is rumbling under the surface, and we've only begun to understand how to release it safely. It took many generations for the church to organize its beliefs into a shame culture. And it will take considerable time for it to change.

Committees: A Healing Asset

Social psychologists suggest that shame can be reduced by cooperative activity. You may already have a clue about this reality. When people are asked to do a task *together,* they find ways to reduce their fear of one another. Get a group of people to play a game and watch their barriers fall. Get a group working on a common task, and despite their differences, they will gain an appreciation of each other. Doing things in teams is a particular strength of the church. Remember all of the jokes you have heard about church committees in heaven? When used in a positive way, church committees have the power to bring diverse people into contact with one another. People sharing a task often share the content of their hearts. All of us live with joys and fears about personal disclosure. All of us cover up feelings of inadequacy in different ways. Working together, we cannot keep up too many pretenses. We are invited through a project, a sharing group, and a prayer meeting in someone's home to become more human and vulnerable. The foundation of most congregations is this process of community building. It can be welcoming or cliquish, to be sure, but a focus on welcome will reduce shame.

Melvin Talbert, a United Methodist bishop, described an event that changed his experience of social prejudice. When he was General Secretary of the General Board of Discipleship, Nashville, he went to a national meeting in which the participants knew that part of the agenda was to lessen any stereotypes they might have had of one another. The participants didn't identify themselves to each other at the start of the two-day meeting, nor in the middle of it. The clergy did not identify who they were. The lesbians and gay men didn't disclose that they were lesbians and gay men, though everyone knew that some of the participants were gay. Others didn't disclose their roles in the church, their marital status, their occupation, or any of the usual "handles" by which people are known. At the end of their first day they had hunches about one another. At the very end of the meeting they greeted one another through the identifying labels we are all so used to.

Talbert found that none of the individuals he had pigeonholed were correctly identified. He came away committed to keeping an open mind and avoiding categories. His passion for inclusion has been a hallmark of his ministry. Sharing diverse opinions, beliefs, and experiences is a rare gift that individuals and congregations can provide.

Leaders Set the Stage

What is required of clergy and laity in the church? Leaders must uncover and learn from the sexual shame in their own families. Murray Bowen, noted psychiatrist and founder of family systems therapy, suggests that healers must learn to heal their own family issues before they can be effective for others. His development of the model of family therapy, now taught widely, includes a concept he refers to as "individuation." One thesis of the Murray Bowen theory is that people who can relate to their families without becoming overwhelmed by their underlying emotional contents are "individuating." In this model people become healthier by staying as unique and different as they may be, while at the same time refusing to be cut off either emotionally or literally from the family system. This theory, applied to life in the church, means that leaders who can fully be themselves and stay connected to people who may be radically different from themselves will effectively ward off shame.[3]

Leaders who assert their rights to be themselves in profoundly confident ways can begin to affect the emotional system. These people can reconnect with others in ways previously thought intolerable. If leaders fear that they will be swallowed up in the emotional mass of the church culture or if they fear that they will be manipulated into thoughts and behaviors that they do not hold, they aren't likely to stay connected. When leaders are strong enough to withstand the pressure to conform, they will likely be able to establish and maintain loving, boundary-centered relationships.

Looking to Jesus

It is time to let Jesus lead us out of shaming and feeling ashamed. See him with the woman who is about to be stoned for committing adultery. Watch the angry flash of his eyes when he says to the crowd, "Let anyone among you who is without sin be the first to throw a stone at her" (John 8:4). Her shame is released by his comment. All of those in the crowd had committed at least one sin. I wonder, too, what happened to the man she had been with. I seethe with the injustice of his escape from shame and persecution at the hands of an angry crowd. But I do know one thing more. The man who wasn't brought before them never heard Jesus' redemptive voice. He carried his shame onward, and perhaps it made him as sour and twisted as the Reverend Tindale became in *The Scarlet Letter*.

Again, see Jesus lifting shame as he tells the story of the prodigal son's welcome home. The young man has "squandered his property in dissolute living" (Luke 15:13). Note that there is nothing in the text that suggests he has been sexually promiscuous; that was an assumption of interpreters in an attempt to make him seem even more immoral. In any event, the man has returned home unemployed and penniless. When "he came to himself," he realized that he had been free to leave home and now he was free to return. His words to his father reflect his shame: "I have sinned against heaven, and before you; I am no longer worthy to be called your son" (Luke 15:18, 19). The father's response was so genuine and loving that the son's shame was erased. The father lavished his son with a robe, sandals, and a ring. He held a great feast in his son's honor. His son had been "dead" in his shame but was restored to a place of life and celebration.

See Jesus with the woman with the flow of blood (Mark 5:25). This woman had been labeled "unclean" for years and years. She had sought help and not found any sympathy or any cure. Jesus didn't worry about his own tarnished image as a result of her touch. He stopped for her, he looked into her eyes, and he healed her of her all-encompassing shame.

See Jesus with Mary at Bethany. She poured a very costly ointment onto Jesus' feet and wiped them with her hair (John 12:3-4; Matt. 26:6-13; Mark 14:3-9). And those around the scene, together with the commentators of the past two thousand years, sneered at her for wasting the costly oil and for her sensual act. The folklore of the Christian church has placed a stigma on this woman, like the other women in these stories. Jesus is adamant that the others stop shaming her. He reports a long list of the ways that his host had not provided for him but that the woman had provided for him. He forgave her for her supposed sins—simply expressed, simply erased.

Every time Jesus heals someone in the Scriptures, two things take place: they are offered grace, and they are restored to community. The leper had been banished by the church because of his contagious illness. Many gay men, lesbians, bisexuals, and transgendered people have felt the sting of this kind of banishment from church, workplace, housing, and community. Jesus tells the leper to be healed and to go back to tell the priest about it. In this act Jesus set the stage for the outcast to confront the church with the healing truth.

Whenever Jesus offered physical healing, he also brought people back into community. Fathers and sons, mothers and daughters are reunited. The physically disabled are healed, but they are also brought back into fellowship with others. The blind man is freed from the accusation by his community that he had sinned. His shame is lifted. His parents' shame is lifted.

Jesus went about lifting shame off of people. The Samaritan woman is invited to converse with him and to satisfy his thirst. Her past life is simply noted. He asks her to change, and she does. Not through his shaming of her, not through her having to feel unworthy, rather through her acceptance of his respect of her. His respectful correction of her behavior didn't brand her as unworthy for use in the life of discipleship. She went on to convert many in her community. She could not have done that had she continued to feel ashamed.

Jesus lifted the tax collectors' shame, the stigma from the mentally ill. He restored the dead and the living dead by pronouncing them worthy of grace and love.

The last act of Jesus on the cross was also an act of shame lifting. The thief hung at Jesus' side, and his conversation with the suffering Messiah redeemed him in a way that no swift pardon for his crime could have. He became a man who had sinned rather than a hopeless sinner. His action was problematic. His identity was cherished. Jesus welcomed him in paradise.

Jesus did not shame others. Nor was Jesus ultimately defeated by shame. He was brutalized, stripped, and hung upon wooden planks. The authorities tried to stop him with shame. But he was not defeated by it. When love and truth are spoken and lived, there is only resurrection.

Questions for Reflection

1. Consider what you and your congregation could do to raise your congregation's self-esteem.
2. Do you agree that "one of things we don't know is that we aren't stuck"?

3. Devise a plan to affirm each other in your small group and/or congregation.
4. Discuss ways that Jesus has shown grace in your life, family, or congregation.
5. Sing "Amazing Grace" together.

Epilogue: The Unbinding

Jesus told them plainly, "Lazarus is dead. . . . Let us go to him."
When Jesus arrived, he found that Lazarus had already been in
the tomb four days. When Martha heard that Jesus was coming, she went and met him. . . . [She said to him] "Lord, if you
had been here, my brother would not have died. But even now
I know that God will give you whatever you ask of him." Jesus
said to her, "Your brother will rise again."

[Jesus asked them,] "Where have you laid him?" They said to
him, "Lord, come and see." Jesus began to weep.

Then Jesus, again greatly disturbed, came to the tomb. It was
a cave, and a stone was lying against it. Jesus said, "Take away
this stone." Martha, the sister of the dead man, said to him,
"Lord, already there is a stench because he has been dead four
days." Jesus said to her, "Did I not tell you that if you believed,
you would see the glory of God?" So they took away the stone.
And Jesus looked upward and said, "Father, I thank you for
having heard me. I knew that you always hear me, but I have
said this for the sake of the crowd standing here, so that they
may believe that you sent me." When he had said this, he cried
with a loud voice, "Lazarus, come out!"

The dead man came out, his hands and feet bound with strips
of cloth, and his face wrapped in a cloth. Jesus said to them,
"Unbind him, and let him go." (John 11:14-44)

I met a man I'll call "Lazarus." I'll call his wife "Martha." They
came into my office for marital therapy. They were bound in shame.

He was in his mid-forties, and the gray hair at his temples
blended with the ashen color of his skin. They had been inti-
mately bound for nearly two decades. He had announced that
their marriage was over. She sat clinging to the pillows of my
overstuffed couch. I watched him as he wrapped his defenses
around himself slowly, methodically. They were the strips of a
dead man's shroud. No embalmer's oil could mask the odor of the
death of their marriage.

The wife was exhausted from crying. She, like the biblical Martha, cried, "Lord, if you had been here, my brother would not have died" (John 11:21). The "if only's" expressed her rage. Where was Jesus when her husband began a new relationship with a woman at his office? Why did the marriage fail? She asked, "If Jesus was with us when we said our wedding vows, what happened to the blessing?" She pleaded with her husband: "Please don't throw away these years without giving me a chance to work on it with you." His reply was this: "If you love me, you'll let me go." She couldn't stop him.

Not only was her husband dead to her, but she faced a death within herself. They were both enshrouded. The husband wore the shroud of deceit, the cloud of shame from his own ugly childhood, and a cloud of shame from an earlier affair. He had inherited shame from his mother, who had been abandoned by his father when she was pregnant. He knew this by hearsay; she never spoke of it. They had all protected this family secret.

The wife also wore a shroud of shame that she had inherited from her father's secret life of affairs in his marriage. She felt deeply flawed and unlovable. She too was bound in the wrappings of shame and had the stench of a shroud around her. The marriage was over.

She continued in therapy. For a long time she was consumed by grief. She sat in her own tomb and wept. For weeks nothing could reach in far enough to touch her pain. Her daily Bible reading was useless. It seemed to me that she was like Martha in John's story; she was aware of the words of her faith. She longed for resurrection but resented that it was taking so long for Jesus to arrive.

While she was weeping one morning in her room, Jesus gently met her and wept with her. And then the weeping stopped. She began, as Lazarus had, to emerge from the tomb. Her bindings began to come loose. Some of it happened in ordinary ways as she reshaped her life as a single person. She stripped the bed of its linens and bought new ones with bright flowers. The comforter was dry-cleaned so that it wouldn't smell like an old memory anymore. She pulled his pictures from her photo albums.

While the external world was reshaped, the inner bindings loosened. She began unwrapping herself, one layer at a time, never sure what would lie in the layer underneath. Yet each deeper layer exposed the distortions and the purity of her lovability. I watched her emerge from the stench of old shame and into the light, where she rejoined her family and friends and was resurrected.

The Scriptures say that it is the community that has the task of unbinding the shame-bound. When Lazarus emerged, Jesus looked at all those who were standing around covering their noses and said, "Unbind him!" They were standing as far back as possible until that moment. He asked them to move in close enough to touch those rotting, stinking cloths and to unwrap the man. The unwrapping of shame involves individual soul searching and the courage of a community of people to come close enough to get involved.

The unbound life is available to us all. What would the unbound life look like for you? Would you need to let go of past wounds within your marriage or partnership or as a single person? Would you need to tell the truth and stop letting a family secret ooze shame for you or your children or grandchildren? Would you need to unwrap yourself from obligations to work or your budget that keep you from your passions? Would you have to go back to school in the middle of your life? Would you have to let go of self-hatred and self-shame? I asked a client what she thought her guilt and shame did for her, and without any pause for deep thought, she shocked herself with her answer. It flew right out. "Without beating myself up with shame," she said, "I'd have to change."

And Jesus said, "I am the resurrection and the life." Unwrap yourselves. Live your life unbound.

Selected Bibliography

Albers, Robert H. 1995. *Shame: A Faith Perspective*. New York: Haworth.

Banmen, John. 1988. "Guilt and Shame: Theories and Therapeutic Possibilities." *International Journal for the Advancement of Counseling* 11:1.

Berecz, John M., and Herbert W. Helm Jr. 1998. "Shame: The Underside of Christianity." *Journal of Psychology and Christianity* 17:1.

Bradshaw, John. 1988. *Healing the Shame That Binds You*. Deerfield Beach, Fla.: Heal.

Fossum, Merle A., and Marilyn J. Mason. 1986. *Facing Shame: Families in Recovery*. New York: Norton.

Friedman, Edwin H. 1985. *Generation to Generation: Family Process in Church and Synagogue*. New York: Guilford.

Goffman, Erving. 1963. *Stigma: Notes on the Management of Spoiled Identity*. Englewood Cliffs, N.J.: Prentice-Hall.

Goldberg, Carl. 1991. *Understanding Shame*. Northvale, N.J.: Aronson.

Imber-Black, Evan. 1993. *Secrets in Families and Family Therapy*. New York: Bantam.

———. 1998. *The Secret Life of Families*. New York: Bantam.

Kaufman, Gershen. 1996. *The Psychology of Shame: Theory and Treatment of Shame-Based Syndromes*. New York: Springer.

Kaufman, Gershen, and Lev Raphael. 1996. *Coming Out of Shame: Transforming Gay and Lesbian Lives*. New York: Doubleday.

McClintock, Karen A. 1998. "Why Is Homosexuality So Hard to Talk About?" in Beth Ann Gaede, ed., *Congregations Talking about Homosexuality*. Minneapolis: Alban Institute.

Neisen, Joseph H. 1993. "Healing from Cultural Victimization: Recovery from Shame Due to Heterosexism." *The Journal of Gay and Lesbian Psychotherapy* 2:1.

Osherson, Samuel, and Steven Kurgman. 1990. "Men, Shame, and Psychotherapy," *Psychotherapy* 27:3.

Osterman, Mary Jo. 1997. *Claiming the Promise: An Ecumenical Welcoming Bible Study Resource on Homosexuality.* Chicago: Reconciling Congregation Program. Available from the National Council on Churches, 3801 N. Keeler Ave., Chicago, IL 60641; (773) 736-5526.

Piers, Gerhart, and Milton B. Singer. 1971. *Shame and Guilt: A Psychoanalytic and a Cultural Study.* New York: Norton.

Schenk, Roy U., and John Everingham. 1995. *Men Healing Shame: An Anthology.* New York: Springer.

Schneider, Carl D. 1992. *Shame, Exposure, and Privacy.* New York: Norton.

Sidoli, Mara. 1988. "Shame and the Shadow." *Journal of Analytical Psychology* 33.

Smedes, Lewis B. 1993. *Shame and Grace: Healing the Shame We Don't Deserve.* San Francisco: HarperSanFrancisco.

Taylor, Gabriele. 1985. *Pride, Shame and Guilt: Emotions of Self-assessment.* Oxford, Eng.: Clarendon, and New York: Oxford University Press.

Thompson, J. Earl, Jr. 1996. "Shame in Pastoral Psychotherapy." *Pastoral Psychology* 44:5..

Whitehead, Evelyn E., and James D. Whitehead. 1994. *A Sense of Sexuality: Christian Love and Intimacy.* New York: Crossroad.

Wink, Walter, ed. 1999. *Homosexuality and Christian Faith: Questions of Conscience for the Churches.* Minneapolis: Fortress Press.

Wurmser, Leon. 1987. *The Mask of Shame.* Baltimore, Md.: Johns Hopkins University Press.

Zaslav, Mark R. 1988. "Shame-Related States of Mind in Psychotherapy." *Journal of Psychotherapy Practice and Research* 7:2.

Notes

Preface

1. Gershen Kaufman, *The Psychology of Shame: Theory and Treatment of Shame-Based Syndromes* (New York: Springer, 1989) 24.

Introduction

1. Leon Wurmser, *The Mask of Shame* (Baltimore, Md.: Johns Hopkins University Press, 1987).

1. Living on the Fault Line

1. James Nelson, The Earl Lectures (Berkeley, Calif.: Pacific School of Religion, January 1994).

2. Center for the Prevention of Sexual and Domestic Violence, 936 N. 34th St., Suite 200, Seattle, Washington 98103; (206) 634-1903.

3. Matthew Fox, audiotaped lecture.

4. Ira L. Reiss, "Society and Sexuality: A Sociological Explanation," in Kathleen McKinney and Susan Sprecher, eds., *Human Sexuality: The Societal and Interpersonal Context*, vol. 14 (Norwood, N.J.: Ablex, 1989), 11.

5. Ibid., 11–12.

6. John Bradshaw, *Healing the Shame That Binds You* (Deerfield Beach, Fla.: Heal Communications, 1988).

7. While most churches do not regularly include sexuality education in their Sunday school programs, there are some exceptions. A series of sexuality education curricula for youth and adults, *Our Whole Lives*, was developed by the Unitarian Universalist Association (UUA) and the United Church of Christ and uses a holistic approach to sexuality. It focuses on helping individuals make responsible decisions based on their faith and values. *Our Whole Lives* is available through the UUA bookstore. For more information, see the UUA Web site: http://www.uua.org/owl.

2. Defining Sexual Shame

1. Evelyn E. Whitehead and James D. Whitehead, *A Sense of Sexuality: Christian Love and Intimacy* (New York: Crossroad, 1994), 45.

2. W. C. Fields, in Clifton Fadiman, ed., *The Little, Brown Book of Anecdotes* (Boston: Little, Brown, 1985), 207.

3. William Masters, Virginia Johnson, and Robert C. Kolodny, *Human Sexuality*, 4th ed. (New York: Harper Collins, 1992), 386.

4. Pamphlet about children of gay and lesbian parents, from Children of Lesbians and Gays Everywhere (COLAGE), 3543 18th St., no. 17, San Francisco, CA 94110.

5. Michael D. Storms, "Theories of Sexual Orientation," in Paul D. Murray, ed., *Lesbian and Gay Studies* (New York: McGraw-Hill, 1998). For information on bisexuality, see Loraine Hutchins and Lani Ka'ahumanu, eds., *Bi Any Other Name: Bisexual People Speak Out* (Boston: Alyson, 1991).

6. See Richard R. Troiden, "Becoming Homosexual: A Model of Gay Identity Acquisition," in Murray, ed., *Lesbian and Gay Studies*, and Stephen F. Morin, *Heterosexual Bias in Psychological Research on Lesbianism and Male Homosexuality* (Washington, D.C.: American Psychological Association, 1977).

7. See Robert H. Albers, *Shame: A Faith Perspective* (New York: Haworth, 1995); John Bradshaw, *Healing the Shame That Binds You* (Deerfield Beach, Fla.: Heal, 1988); and Lewis B. Smedes, *Shame and Grace: Healing the Shame We Don't Deserve* (San Francisco: Harper-SanFrancisco, 1993).

8. Henry Ward, "Shame: A Necessity for Growth in Therapy," *American Journal of Psychotherapy* 26, 2 (1972): 232–43.

9. Mark R. Zaslav, "Shame-Related States of Mind in Psychotherapy," *Journal of Psychotherapy Practice and Research* 7, 2 (1988): 157.

10. Gershen Kaufman, *The Psychology of Shame: Theory and Treatment of Shame-Based Syndromes* (New York: Springer, 1996), 147.

11. Zaslav, "Shame-Related States," 155.

12. Ibid.

13. Merle A. Fossum and Marilyn J. Mason, *Facing Shame: Families in Recovery* (New York: Norton, 1986), 6.

14. Kaufman, *Psychology of Shame*, 24.

15. Ibid.

16. Ibid.

17. Henri Nouwen in personal conversation with Rev. Martha (Martie) McMane and Rev. Alan Johnson.

18. Kaufman, *Psychology of Shame*, 26.

19. Silvan S. Tomkins, *Affect, Imagery, Consciousness: The Negative Affects: Anger and Fear* (New York: Springer, 1991).

20. Kaufman, *Psychology of Shame*, 121.

21. Tomkins, *Affect*, 270.

22. Kaufman, *Psychology of Shame*, 127.

3. Major Shifts in the Study of Human Sexuality

1. Alfred C. Kinsey, Wardell B. Pomeroy, and Clyde E. Martin, *Sexual Behavior in the Human Male* (Philadelphia: Saunders, 1948).

2. Kurt Hass and Adelaide Hass, *Understanding Sexuality* (St. Louis: Mosby, 1993), 37.

4. Judeo-Christian Sexuality

1. L. William Countryman, *Dirt, Greed, and Sex: Sexual Ethics in the New Testament and Their Implications for Today* (Minneapolis: Fortress, 1998).

2. Ibid., 243.

3. Ibid., 244.

4. Robert H. Albers, *Shame: A Faith Perspective* (New York: Haworth, 1995), 89.

5. Reay Tannahill, *Sex in History* (New York: Stein and Day, 1980), 141.

6. Evelyn E. Whitehead and James D. Whitehead, *A Sense of Sexuality: Christian Love and Intimacy* (New York: Crossroad, 1994), 97.

7. Ibid., 136–39.

8. Sam Keen, *The Passionate Life: Stages of Loving* (San Francisco: Harper & Row, 1983), 9.

9. See the Web site of the ACLU: http://www.aclu.org/issues/gay/sodomy.html.

10. James A. Haught, "Sex and God; Is Religion Twisted?" *The Free Inquiry* (fall 1977).

11. Reported in *Shalom to You* 7, 10 (October 1999). *Shalom to You* is the newsletter of Shalom Ministries: A United Methodist Ministry of Empowerment, Education, and Justice, P. O. Box 66147, Portland, OR 97290.

12. *The United Methodist Book of Discipline* (Nashville: United Methodist Publishing House, 1996), par. 65G.

5. Sexual Sin

1. Donald Goergen, *The Sexual Celibate* (New York: Seabury, 1975), 75.

2. George Bernard Shaw, cited by Albert Benschop, editor of the University of Amsterdam's sociology Web site (1996): http:// www.pscw.uva.nl/sociosite.

3. Matt Groening, "Basic Sex Facts for Today's Youngfolk," *Life In Hell* (comic strip).

4. Lee Ellis and M. Ashley Ames, "Neurohormonal Functioning and Sexual Orientation: A Theory of Homosexuality–Heterosexuality," in Paul D. Murray, ed., *Lesbian and Gay Studies* (New York: McGraw-Hill, 1998).

5. Gershen Kaufman and Lev Raphael, *Coming Out of Shame: Transforming Gay and Lesbian Lives* (New York: Doubleday, 1996).

6. Virginia Ramey Mollenkott, *Women, Men and the Bible* (New York: Crossroad, 1988).

7. David R. Mace, *The Christian Response to the Sexual Revolution* (Nashville: Abingdon, 1987).

8. Leo Buscaglia, *Loving Relationships* (Sacramento, Calif.: KVIE for PBS Video, 1984).

9. Ogden Nash, *Zoo* (New York: Workman, 1987).

10. United Church Board of Homeland Ministries, *Human Sexuality: A Preliminary Study* (New York: United Church Press, 1977), 104.

11. *Peggy Sue Got Married*, Tri-Star Pictures, 1986.

6. Revisiting the Garden

1. John M. Berecz and Herbert W. Helm Jr., "Shame: The Underside of Christianity," *Journal of Psychology and Christianity* 17, 1 (spring 1998): 5–14.

2. Renita J. Weems, "Commentary on Song of Songs," *The New Interpreters' Bible*, vol. 5 (Nashville: Abingdon, 1997), 364.

3. Evelyn E. Whitehead and James D. Whitehead, *A Sense of Sexuality: Christian Love and Intimacy* (New York: Crossroad, 1994), 95.

4. Weems, "Commentary on Song of Songs," 370.

5. See Carey Ellen Walsh, *Exquisite Desire: Religion, the Erotic, and the Song of Songs* (Minneapolis: Fortress Press, 2000); Rosemary Radford Ruether, *Sexism and God-Talk: Toward a Feminist Theology* (Boston: Beacon Press, 1983); Marvin Pope, *Commentary on the Song of Songs*, Anchor Bible Series vol. 7 (Garden City, N.Y.: Doubleday, 1977); and Phyllis Trible, "Depatriarchalizing in Biblical Interpretation," *Journal of the American Academy of Religion* 41 (1973): 30–48.

7. Gender and Shame

1. Tertullian, "De Cultu Feminarum 1.1," *The Fathers of the Church*, vol. 40 (Washington, D.C.: Catholic University Press and Consortium Books, 1977), 177f.

2. Sigmund Freud, "The Origin and Development of Psycho-analysis," in *A General Selection from the Works of Sigmund Freud,* ed. John Rickman (New York: Anchor/Doubleday, 1989), 9.

3. "While it has been argued that women are shame prone (Lewis 1971), we have come to believe that men are more shame vulnerable. Shame . . . plays a critical and largely unrecognized role in the formation and on-going organization of the male character" (Samuel Osherson and Steven Kurgman, "Men, Shame, and Psychotherapy," *Psychotherapy* 27, 3 [1990]: 327).

4. Roy Schenk and John Everingham, eds., *Men Healing Shame: An Anthology* (New York: Springer, 1995), 41.

5. For information on transgender identity, see Kate Bornstein, *Gender Outlaw: On Men, Women, and the Rest of Us* (New York: Vintage Books, 1994).

6. *Ma Vie en Rose,* Haute et Courte, Sony Picture Classics and Columbia Tri-Star, 1997.

7. Shmuley Boteach, "Free at Last," *London Times* (1999).

8. When the Pastor Is Ashamed

1. Alexander Lowen, *Narcissism: Denial of the True Self* (New York: Macmillan, 1985), 9.

2. *The Collected Papers of Sigmund Freud,* vol. 4, ed. Ernest Jones (New York: Basic, 1953), 32.

3. Edwin H. Friedman, *Generation to Generation: Family Process in Church and Synagogue* (New York: Guilford, 1985), 220–49.

4. John M. Berecz and Herbert W. Helm Jr., "Shame: The Underside of Christianity," *Journal of Psychology and Christianity* 17, 1 (spring 1998): 8–9.

9. Individual Shame and the Congregation

1. Edwin H. Friedman, *Generation to Generation: Family Process in Church and Synagogue* (New York: Guilford, 1985), 70.

10. The Rules

1. Karen A. McClintock, "Why Is Homosexuality So Hard to Talk About?" in Beth Ann Gaede, ed., *Congregations Talking about Homosexuality* (Minneapolis: Alban Institute, 1998).

2. To further illustrate the ways in which congregations experience and perpetuate shame, I am borrowing from the work of family therapists Merle A. Fossum, ACSW, and Marilyn J. Mason, Ph.D. Fossum and Mason work with the Family Therapy Institute

in St. Paul, Minnesota. In their book, *Facing Shame: Families in Recovery* (New York: Norton, 1986), they draw on their experience as family therapists using systems theory to illustrate the damage of shame in family systems.

3. Mary Jo Osterman, *Claiming the Promise: An Ecumenical Welcoming Bible Study Resource on Homosexuality* (Chicago: Reconciling Congregation Program, 1997) 24.

4. Fossum and Mason, *Facing Shame*, 26.

5. John Boswell, "Subsequent Developments: A Look Forward," in Paul D. Murray, ed., *Lesbian and Gay Studies* (New York: McGraw-Hill, 1998), 1–12.

6. James Nelson, *Embodiment: An Approach to Sexuality and Christian Theology* (Minneapolis: Augsburg, 1978), 14.

11. Sexual Identity Shame

1. Joseph H. Neisen, "Healing from Cultural Victimization: Recovery from Shame Due to Heterosexism," *Journal of Gay and Lesbian Psychotherapy* 2, 1 (1993): 49–63.

2. Ibid.

3. Written notes prepared for a witness in worship (1999). For the purpose of this book, the author wishes to remain anonymous.

4. For a full look at the healing of homosexual shame, I recommend Gershen Kaufman and Lev Raphael, *Coming Out of Shame: Transforming Gay and Lesbian Lives* (New York: Doubleday, 1996).

5. To contact PFLAG's national office, write PFLAG, 1012 14th St. N.W., Suite 700, Washington, DC 20005, or call (202) 638-4200. Call their publishing branch for an excellent bibliography of resources: 800-621-6969. Or go to their Web site: http://www.pflag.org.

6. Karen A. McClintock, "Children of the Closet: A Measurement of the Anxiety and Self-Esteem of Children Raised by a Nondisclosed Homosexual or Bisexual Parent" (Ph.D. diss., Union Institute, Cincinnati, Ohio, 2000).

7. A national support network for children of gay, lesbian, bisexual, and transgender parents is Children of Lesbians and Gays Everywhere (COLAGE), 3543 18th St., no. 17, San Francisco, CA 94110; (415) 861-5437; e-mail: colage@colage.org.

12. Shame and Culture

1. Gabriele Taylor, *Pride, Shame and Guilt: Emotions of Self-Assessment* (Oxford, Eng.: Clarendon, and New York: Oxford University Press, 1985), 57.

2. Gershen Kaufman, *The Psychology of Shame: Theory and Treatment of Shame-Based Syndromes* (New York: Springer, 1989), 44.

3. Evelyn E. Whitehead and James D. Whitehead, *Shadows of the Heart: A Spirituality of the Painful Emotions* (New York: Crossroad, 1998), 150.

4. Nathaniel Hawthorne, *The Scarlet Letter: A Romance* (New York: Penguin, 1983), 89.

5. Lewis B. Smedes, *Shame and Grace: Healing the Shame We Don't Deserve* (San Francisco: HarperSanFrancisco, 1993), 80.

6. John M. Berecz and Herbert W. Helm Jr., "Shame: The Underside of Christianity," *Journal of Psychology and Christianity* 17, 1 (spring 1998): 9.

7. Robert H. Albers, *Shame: A Faith Perspective* (New York: Haworth, 1995), 70.

8. Elizabeth Clephane, "Beneath the Cross of Jesus," in *United Methodist Hymnal* (Nashville: United Methodist Publishing, 1989).

9. See Rita Nakashima Brock, *Journeys by Heart: A Christology of Erotic Power* (New York: Crossroad, 1992), or Joanne Carlson Brown and Carole R. Bohn, eds., *Christianity, Patriarchy, and Abuse: A Feminist Critique* (New York: Pilgrim, 1989).

10. Smedes, *Shame and Grace*, 46.

•11. Flora Wuellner, *Release for Trapped Christians* (New York: Abingdon, 1974).

13. Methods of Healing

1. Elliot Aronson, *The Social Animal*, 7th ed. (New York: Freeman, 1996), 336–43.

14. Ground Rules for Conversations

1. Merle A. Fossum and Marilyn J. Mason, *Facing Shame: Families in Recovery* (New York: Norton, 1986).

15. Lifting the Shame

1. Morris Rosenberg, *Society and the Adolescent Self-Image* (Princeton, N.J.: Princeton University Press, 1965).

2. Lewis B. Smedes, *Shame and Grace: Healing the Shame We Don't Deserve* (San Francisco: HarperSanFrancisco, 1993), 147.

3. Murray Bowen, *Family Therapy in Clinical Practice* (New York: Aronson, 1978).